Caroling Through Advent and Christmas

Daily Reflections with Familiar Hymns

Mark G. Boyer

Liguori

Dedicated to Michael King,
a lifelong friend

Imprimi Potest:
Harry Grile, CSsR, Provincial
Denver Province, The Redemptorists

Published by Liguori Publications
Liguori, Missouri 63057

To order, visit Liguori.org or call 800-325-9521.

Cataloging-in-Publication Data is on file with the Library of Congress

p ISBN: 978-0-7648-2524-8
e ISBN: 978-0-7648-6968-6

The Scripture quotations contained herein are from the *New Revised Standard Version Bible: Catholic Edition* copyright © 1993 and 1989 by the Division of Christian Education of the National Council of the Churches of Christ in the USA. Used by permission. All rights reserved.

The texts of the hymns contained herein are in the public domain. They may be published and otherwise reproduced without permission. Most of them are taken from *Resource Collection of Hymns and Service Music for the Liturgy,* copyright © 1981 by International Committee on English in the Liturgy, Inc., and published by G.I.A. Publications, Inc., 7404 South Mason Ave., Chicago, IL 60638. Also, they can be found in worship aids, hymnals, online, and in many other collections of hymns and carols.

Liguori Publications, a nonprofit corporation, is an apostolate of The Redemptorists. To learn more about The Redemptorists, visit Redemptorists.com.

Printed in the United States of America
18 17 16 15 14 / 5 4 3 2 1
First Edition

Table of Contents

Introduction

The loss of an hour of daylight on the first Sunday of November signals the near-end of fall and the onset of winter. There are leaves to rake, water hoses to store, and lots of other things to do before the jet stream sends the first blast of Arctic air across the continent. In the colder environment, the sunrise pink seems to be pinker and the gray streaks grayer.

While nature is observing the change of seasons, so is the Catholic Church. The last Sunday of November or the first Sunday of December heralds a new liturgical year of grace. All things begin again. The ribbon at the back of *The Roman Missal* gets moved to the front. The marker in the *Lectionary* goes to the obverse of the book and a new cycle of Scripture texts begins. We see a fresh Advent wreath with three violet candles and one rose candle in church; each torch awaits the fire that will set it ablaze as the solemn season prepares us for the great Christmas feast. As the days decrease in light, we ignite candles on a wreath that point us toward the light of Christ. In other words, newness and light permeate Advent with the fresh scent of newly harvested greens and beeswax—and with the sounds of the seasons.

One of the many things we do as Roman Catholics is sing Advent hymns and Christmas carols. During Advent we express in song our longing for Christ to come in glory even as we prepare to mark his Nativity on December 25. Sometime in November, or commonly as early as October, Christmas songs are heard in shopping malls, in discount stores, on the radio, on TV, and through all manner of electronic devices. The secular form of Christmas is characterized by its own music, just like the religious seasons of Advent and Christmas have their own hymns and carols. We take time to observe up to four weeks of Advent so that our even-shorter observance of Christmas will be enriched with God's word, prayer, and singing.

We may catch ourselves humming an Advent hymn that we heard in church on Sunday, especially the old standby: "O Come, O Come, Emmanuel." Or we might create a joyful chorus, joining the other members of our family in singing a verse of an Advent hymn. Likewise, after observing the solemn Advent season, we sing alone a joyous Christmas carol or join others in narrating in song the birth, epiphany, and baptism of Jesus Christ.

This book presents an exercise for every day of Advent and Christmas that combines the daily Scripture texts from the Lectionary for Mass with religious hymns sung during the Advent season and carols chorused during the Christmas season. The hymns and carols used in this book should be familiar to most Catholics. If not, search for their titles or lyrics online; in most cases recordings by modern musicians in various styles can be found and listened to.

This book can be used by individuals for private prayer or by families and groups. A six-part exercise is offered for each entry:

1   The liturgical day is given, such as Monday of the first week of Advent. To determine the specific date for a liturgical day, a Catholic calendar can be consulted.

2   The daily Mass readings from the Lectionary for Mass are listed. The reader is urged to review them by reading them from his or her Bible before continuing. If this book is being used for family devotion, various members of the family can take turns reading the assigned passages. For Sundays with readings for Cycles A, B, and C, keep in mind that the new liturgical year begins with the first Sunday of Advent. Church Year 2015 (Advent 2014) uses Cycle B. Cycle C begins with Advent 2015, Cycle A with Advent 2016, and so on.

3   A verse from a traditional hymn or religious carol is presented. All the lyrics of the hymns and carols used are in the public domain. If the reader knows the music for the hymn or carol, he or she is encouraged to sing it or hum it to himself or herself or to sing it as a family.

4   A reflection follows. The reflection is based on the biblical texts and the verse from the carol or hymn in the context of the liturgical seasons of Advent or Christmas. The individual may read the reflection, or one person of a family may read it aloud for others.

5   Throughout the reflections I use the masculine pronoun for God, Lord, Lord God, etc. I am well aware that God is neither male nor female, but to avoid the repetition of nouns over and over again, I employ male pronouns, as they are also used throughout most biblical translations.

6   The reflection is followed by a question for personal meditation. The question functions as a guide for personal appropriation of the message of the reflection, and, hopefully, leads the reader into deeper prayer. After a few minutes of reflection, family members may want to share their thoughts about the question.

7   A prayer concludes the exercise and summarizes the theme explored in the reflection and will serve as the foundation for the meditation. One member of a family may say the prayer for all, or all may proclaim the prayer together.

Every year the Advent and Christmas seasons look a little different, so it should be noted that every entry presented here will not always be used. When the Advent season is shortened (because Christmas is early in the week), the Christmas season is lengthened. When the Advent season occupies all four weeks (and Christmas falls on Sunday), the Christmas season is shortened. Thus, not all of the entries for the third week of Advent will normally be used. At least one, and usually several, of the entries for January 2 through January 7 will be omitted because the Solemnity of the Epiphany of the Lord will be celebrated on the Sunday between January 2 and January 8. Some, and in a few years all, of the entries following January 8 will be omitted because the feast of the Baptism of the Lord is marked on the Monday after Epiphany instead of on the following Sunday. The best way to know which entry to use is to follow a Catholic calendar.

It is my hope that these entries will enable you to carol your way through Advent and Christmas and come to both a deeper relationship with God and a renewed appreciation for these weeks of the liturgical year.

Fr. Mark G. Boyer

Section I:
First Week of Advent

On Sundays during Advent and Christmas there will be three reflections to accompany the yearly cycles as noted in the introduction. Choose the reflection that accompanies the current year's readings: Cycle A, B, or C.

First Sunday of Advent, *Cycle A*

Scriptures: Isaiah 2:1–5; Romans 13:11–14; Matthew 24:37–44

Hymn

Go, tell it on the mountain,
Over the hills and ev'ry where;
Go, tell it on the mountain
That Jesus Christ is born.
Down in a lowly manger
The humble Christ was born,
And God sent us salvation
That blessed Christmas morn.

"Go, Tell It on the Mountain," verse 4

Reflection

"Go, tell it on the mountain" is our song on this first Sunday of Advent. Isaiah records his vision of the mountain of the Lord's house being established as the highest mountain and all people streaming toward Jerusalem to enjoy the everlasting peace of God's kingdom. Paul tells the Romans, salvation is nearer today than when we first believed. Every day that passes brings us closer to the day of Christ's return in glory. We look back to his birth in a lowly manger on Christmas morning even as we look forward to the fullness of salvation when he comes again.

The first two weeks of Advent are focused on preparing ourselves for the Lord's Second Coming. Jesus makes clear in Matthew's Gospel that his arrival will be unexpected, like a thief in the night. As Noah prepared for the flood, we should prepare for Christ's return in glory. While we may question when that day will arrive, during Advent we stand together united in hope to prepare for that day. When the Son of Man comes, those who are prepared will be taken and the unprepared will be left.

During the solemn Advent season, we stop and take inventory of our lives so that we can be prepared for Christ's return in glory. We want to examine our daily prayer rituals to be sure that they have not become routine. We want to pay attention to how well we are living our baptismal promises, renouncing evil, and professing our faith in our triune God. Advent preparation includes less rushing around and more quiet reflection—a stark contrast to our cultural Christmas frenzy. ✠

Meditation

Of the following, which one is your favorite Advent metaphor: mountain climbing, light vs. darkness, prepared vs. unprepared? Explain.

Prayer

Come, Lord Jesus, and do not delay. Grant us the help of the Holy Spirit so that we may be dressed in the armor of light so that at your coming we may enter your kingdom, where you live with the Father and the Holy Spirit, forever and ever. Amen.

First Sunday of Advent, *Cycle B*

Scriptures: Isaiah 63:16b–17, 19b; 64:2–7; 1 Corinthians 1:3–9; Mark 13:33–37

Hymn

Creator of the stars of night,
Your people's everlasting light,
Jesus, Redeemer, save us all,
And hear your servants when they call.

"*Creator of the Stars of Night,*" *verse 1*

Reflection

This first Sunday of Advent should find us watching for Christ's return in glory. Repeatedly, Jesus commands his disciples in Mark's Gospel to watch, be alert, stay awake; he may come early in the morning, at midday, in the afternoon, in the evening, at midnight. Whatever spiritual gifts God has given to us should be employed to shape us like a potter molds clay in awaiting the revelation of the Lord Jesus Christ, writes St. Paul.

Isaiah calls on the creator of the stars, the Lord, to tear the heavens open and come to earth with the mountains quaking before him. The prophet asks this of God so that the people might be saved. The deeds of the Holy One in the past are nothing compared to what is expected in the future when the Lord Jesus Christ will come in glory. No ear has heard the story of what is to come. No eye has seen any God except the Lord preparing his people for the day of his Son's Second Coming.

Stand on tiptoe and look over the windowsill. What imminent expectation do you see? The earth has quietly fallen asleep, yet life is stirring in root and bulb underground. Furry wild animals scurry through yards and trees, expecting to find nuts and berries to satisfy their winter hunger. And people, too, are alert to the weather forecast, especially if it might include ice, snow, or freezing rain. ✠

Meditation

What spiritual gift most molds you into Advent waiting?

Prayer

Father, creator of the stars of night, you are our everlasting light. Keep us watchful and alert for our Redeemer's coming in glory. Hear your servants' call through the same Christ, our Lord. Amen.

First Sunday of Advent, *Cycle C*

Scriptures: Jeremiah 33:14–16; 1 Thessalonians 3:12–4:2; Luke 21:25–28, 34–36

Hymn

Come, thou long expected Jesus,
Born to set thy people free;
From our fears and sins release us;
Let us find our rest in thee.
Israel's strength and consolation,
Hope of all the earth thou art,
Dear desire of ev'ry nation,
Joy of ev'ry longing heart.
"Come, Thou Long Expected Jesus," verse 1

Reflection

Today, the Church begins a period of longing for Christ's return in glory. The first two weeks of Advent do not focus on Jesus' birth in Bethlehem; rather, they are focused on his Second Coming. The first verse of "Come, Thou Long Expected Jesus" expresses this desire well, as does St. Paul in his First Letter to the Thessalonians, urging the Thessalonians to be found holy—in a healthy relationship with God—when Jesus returns.

Jeremiah looks forward to a day when God would raise up a descendant of King David, who would set the people free from fears of foreign domination and, thus, be Israel's hope and consolation. And the Lukan Jesus, whom Christians believe to be the one for whom Jeremiah hoped, urges vigilance for his return in a cloud with great power and glory. During Advent, the hope of the earth and of every nation becomes flesh in those who keep this longing in their hearts. Their joy is tangible as, in the words of the Mass, they await the blessed hope and the coming of their Savior, Jesus Christ.

We hear words about waiting for Christ's return in glory during every Mass. Phrases like "until you [, Lord,] come again," "we look forward to his second coming," "we await his coming in glory," and "looking forward to his blessed Coming" become very familiar. Thinking about them may awaken in us some Advent reflection. ✚

Meditation

In what specific ways do you await the return of Christ in glory?

Prayer

Come, long-expected Jesus, and set us free from fears and sin. Let our longing hearts find rest in you, who are Lord forever and ever. Amen.

Monday of the First Week of Advent

Scriptures:
Year A: Isaiah 4:2–6; Matthew 8:5–11
Years B & C: Isaiah 2:1–5; Matthew 8:5–11

Hymn

To heal the sick stretch out your hand,
And bid the fallen sinner stand;
Shine forth, and let your light restore
Earth's own true loveliness once more.
"On Jordan's Bank the Baptist's Cry," verse 4

Reflection

The Matthean Jesus demonstrates that God's kingdom has come to the earth by healing the Gentile centurion's paralyzed servant because of his master's faith. By stretching out his hand and healing the sick, Jesus fulfills Isaiah's vision of nations streaming to the Lord's mountain. The suffering servant's light is restored. Indeed, a small part of earth's true loveliness is re-created by Jesus.

We don't have to be doctors to bring healing into the world. Greeting a fellow traveler on the bus, train, or subway can soothe a morning that has not gone according to human plans.

Visiting the elderly in nursing homes and bringing them the Eucharist can be a healing touch. Picking up the stray paper dancing in the wind on the sidewalk can heal the earth. Like the Roman centurion, no one is worthy to have

Jesus enter his home, but we can bring him to those who need him most. With the Roman centurion, we Catholics declare our faith at every Mass, saying, "Lord, I am not worthy that you should enter under my roof, but only say the word and my soul shall be healed." ✤

Meditation

In what specific ways do you manifest the kingdom of God by restoring a small part of earth's loveliness?

Prayer

Stretch out your hand, O God, and heal the sick and bid the fallen sinner stand. In us, shine forth your kingdom, and let your light shine forth, restoring earth's true loveliness. Through Christ, our Lord. Amen.

Tuesday of the First Week of Advent

Scriptures: Isaiah 11:1–10; Luke 10:21–24

Hymn

Lo, how a Rose e'er blooming
From tender stem hath sprung!
Of Jesse's lineage coming,
As those of old have sung.
It came a flower bright,
Amid the cold of winter,
When half spent was the night.

"Lo, How a Rose E'er Blooming," verse 1

Reflection

In the midst of the wallpaperesque description in Isaiah of wolves and lambs, leopards and kids, calves and lions, cows and bears, and babies and snakes, Jesus has made it possible for modern people to understand that he has removed all animosity from the earth. Picking up a newspaper or magazine or reading hot news on the internet presents a different story of murder and robbery, deception and lies, rape and violence, poverty and homelessness. Indeed, the Isaiahian wallpaper clashes with the rest of the room.

Experience dictates that Isaiah's idyllic nursery scene has not yet fully come to pass. Yes, the shoot has sprouted from the stump of Jesse and a rosebud has blossomed. Jesus was born 2,000 years ago. The living saints—us—still wait for Christ's return in glory when all will be made new. Daily, we wait in joyful hope as our sighs ascend to

God's throne in heaven. Getting our cue from the Book of Revelation, we pray, "Come!" For 2,000 years we have asked Christ to come.

What was hidden from the wise and the learned has been revealed to the childlike, but an adult world confronts living saints around every corner. All long for justice that defeats wickedness, for faithfulness that slays disloyalty. Seeing the vision and making it a reality is the task at hand during this time of waiting. It takes effort to give others what is due them instead of cheating them. It takes faithfulness to a relationship to protect human dignity rather than using another to get what one wants. Living saints must be vigilant that their faith does not slip into a cultural religion that proclaims it is OK to do whatever one wants. ✠

Meditation

For what do you long or sigh for during Advent?

Prayer

Shoot of Jesse, blossom the Spirit of wisdom and understanding, counsel and strength, knowledge and awe: Confound the wicked by enabling us to act with justice. Come in glory and reveal to us the Father, who lives and reigns with you and the Holy Spirit, one God, forever and ever. Amen.

Wednesday of the First Week of Advent

Scriptures: Isaiah 25:6–10a; Matthew 15:29–37

Hymn

Go, tell it on the mountain,
Over the hills and ev'rywhere;
Go, tell it on the mountain
That Jesus Christ is born.
While shepherds kept their watching
O'er silent flocks by night,
Behold, throughout the heavens
There shone a holy light.

"Go, Tell It on the Mountain," verse 1

Reflection

Creation's second birth is depicted by both Isaiah and Matthew. Isaiah's Lord invites all to Mount Zion, where he spreads a table with rich food and choice wines, where he gives food that destroys death and wipes away tears of mourning. In a word, God saves his people. And that is something to go tell on the mountain.

Matthew's Jesus goes to a mountain and cures the lame, restores sight to the blind, makes the deformed whole, and the mute speak. Then, after saving the crowds, he feeds them with seven loaves and fish, and collects the same number of baskets of leftovers. The holy light of his birth continues to shine through his mighty works.

God desires that all be made new; God wants to satisfy this longing earth—those who desire a few morsels of food, those who pray to have their diseases and ailments transformed into wholeness. It is a longing for a new birth that rises like a river from the core of one's inner being. Such desire for completion is discovered through the metaphors of food and wine, health and wholeness.

Advent's mountain-climbing experience brings all mountaineers closer to the Lord, who saves the hungry from death with the finest food and drink. Daily, the loaves are multiplied at Mass. Daily, the cup is filled with choice wine. Those who dine on the Body and Blood of Christ—on the one who multiplies loaves—are promised eternal life, that is, transformation, newness, second birth, and salvation through God's love. ✤

Meditation

In what specific ways is God saving you?

Prayer
Lord of hosts, we look to you to save us from all that threatens the wholeness for which we long. Give new birth to all your creatures through Christ, your Son, who lives with you and the Holy Spirit, one God, forever and ever. Amen.

Thursday of the First Week of Advent

Scriptures: Isaiah 26:1–6; Matthew 7:21, 24–27

Hymn

Zion hears the watchmen singing,
And all her heart with joy is springing;
She wakes, she rises from her gloom:
For her Lord comes down all glorious,
The strong in grace, in truth victorious,
Her star is ris'n, her light is come.
Now come, O blessed one,
God's own beloved Son; Alleluia!
We follow to the festal hall
To sup with you, the Lord of all.

"Wake, Awake! For Night Is Flying," verse 2

Reflection

The strong city of Isaiah's song is individualized in Jesus' teaching about building a house on rock rather than on sand. The Lord, being an eternal rock, gives the house-builder architectural wisdom, so he establishes his home solidly on rock. The self-made architect is a fool because his house collapses and is completely ruined on sand.

Vigilance is required. In Isaiah's world, watchmen walked and patrolled Zion's walls, often singing during the night, indicating no enemy invasion and peace. The watchmen watched, but they knew that it was God who kept Jerusalem safe; his light removed her gloom. The cry, "Lord, Lord," will not automatically gain entry into the new Zion, the kingdom of heaven. Doing the Father's will, building on rock, is the sure way to protect from the flash floods and the wild winds—modern enemies—that buffet the house.

Architectural wisdom is a gift from God. It enables us to give away what we do not need so that we can build a solid house. Awaiting the coming of the Blessed One, God's own beloved Son, during Advent, we do well to practice charity so that we might enter the festal hall of the new Jerusalem, built on rock, to dine with the God of all. ✠

Meditation

On what or whom is your house built?
How does charity help to open doors?

Prayer

O Lord, eternal rock, protect us from the floods and winds that buffet our homes. Give us peace through our works of charity as we await the coming in glory of your Blessed One, Jesus Christ, your beloved Son, who is Lord forever and ever. Amen.

Friday of the First Week of Advent

Scriptures: Isaiah 29:17–24; Matthew 9:27–31

Hymn

"Wake, awake! For night is flying,"
The watchmen on the heights are crying,
"Awake, Jerusalem, at last!"
Midnight hears the welcome voices,
And at the thrilling cry rejoices:
"Come forth, you virgins, night is past:
The bridegroom comes; awake,
Your lamps with gladness take, Alleluia!
And for his marriage feast prepare,
For you must go to meet him there."

"Wake, Awake! For Night Is Flying," verse 1

Reflection

An image often presented in the season of Advent is that of bride and groom. The bride is the Church—composed of many members—and the groom is Christ, who for whatever reason is delayed arriving at the marriage feast. We should be like the five wise virgins in the parable in Matthew's Gospel. They come forth to greet the bridegroom with lamps alight and enter with him into the marriage feast.

In the words of today's passage from the prophet Isaiah, we should be like an orchard, a place of fruitful life, finding joy in Christ. Our deafness can be turned to hearing, and our blindness to sight by the Son of David, who healed two blind men because of their faith.

The days and nights of Advent fly, while the Scriptures cry that the Lord is coming to enlighten his servants who remain prepared in faithfulness. If we have heard the cry, we should be going forth to meet Christ with a burning lamp in hand.

That lamp is fueled by the oil of our lives. That oil is composed of all the praying we have ever done, all the charity we have ever given, all the work we have shared without pay, all the volunteering we have contributed to a worthy cause. As our lives increase in age, so should the amount of oil in our burning lamps. ✠

Meditation

What characterizes your preparedness for Christ's return in glory?

Prayer

O Lord, our light and our salvation, fill our days and nights with longing for the coming of the Son of David. Prepare us for his marriage feast that we may join Christ in the kingdom, where you live and reign forever and ever. Amen.

Saturday of the First Week of Advent

Scriptures: Isaiah 30:19–21, 23–26;
Matthew 9:35–10:1, 5a, 6–8

Hymn

Hark! The herald angels sing,
"Glory to the new-born King;
Peace on earth and mercy mild,
God and sinners reconciled!"
Joyful, all ye nations rise,
Join the triumph of the skies;
With th'angelic host proclaim:
"Christ is born in Bethlehem!"
Hark! The herald angels sing,
Glory to the new-born King!"

"Hark! The Herald Angels Sing," verse 1

Reflection

God has mild mercy on his people. Jesus shows God's mercy to his people as they prepare for his coming. Isaiah assures his readers that the Holy One of Israel hears and answers their prayers. He demonstrates his faithfulness by providing rain for the sown seed, abundant wheat, spacious meadows for grazing sheep, silage for domesticated animals, and streams of flowing water. Jesus, the Lamb of God, reveals God's mercy by curing diseases and illness and proclaiming the imminence of God's kingdom to the lost sheep of Israel.

Biblical mercy is not cultural mercy, which is characterized as giving another whatever he or she seeks.

Biblical mercy refers to God's faithfulness to the terms of the covenant; the Lord prepares the path and directs his people to walk in it to receive his overflowing blessings. Jesus toured towns and villages dispensing God's blessings and declaring that they proclaimed the presence of God's kingdom for all who would receive them in repentance. In other words, Jesus came to reconcile God and sinners.

As recipients of the Holy One's gifts, we, like those who encountered Jesus, taste the kingdom and await its fullness. During Advent, we wait for the One who was once born in Bethlehem to come in glory. And while we wait, we give away whatever we have received, because we received it without cost. In the kingdom, all gifts are passed from one to another. When we give away what we have received, the angels sing. ✠

Meditation

What gift has God given to you and have you given to another?

Prayer

Lord God, Holy One of Israel, you are gracious when we cry to you for mercy. Gather all your sheep into the kingdom when your Son, Jesus Christ, returns in glory. He is Lord forever and ever. Amen.

Solemnity: The Immaculate Conception of the Blessed Virgin Mary

This Holy Day of Obligation is celebrated every year on December 8, unless the 8th is a Sunday. In the latter case, the solemnity is marked on Monday and the obligation is removed.

Scriptures: Genesis 3:9–15, 20; Ephesians 1:3–6, 11–12; Luke 1:26–38

Hymn

Now grieving that the ancient curse
Should doom to death a universe,
You heal all those who need your grace
And come to save our fallen race.

"Creator of the Stars of Night," verse 2

Reflection

Part of the ancient curse is found in the passage from the Book of Genesis—the curse on the serpent (the curse on the man and the woman are not a part of today's reading). After the man and woman disobeyed their Creator, the universe was doomed to death until Jesus redeemed the fallen race and offered God's grace, the Divine's own life, as healing to all in need.

One woman did not need to be saved. She was destined for adoption through the very Son she conceived. God favored her from the moment of her conception so that she might praise the glory of his grace, which he granted to her through his own beloved Son. That is why the angel Gabriel greets the virgin, saying, "Greetings, favored one!"

(Luke 1:28). The favored one, the full-of-grace one, reverses the ancient curse by striking the serpent's head. She is a new Eve because she became not only the Mother of all the living but because she also gave birth to the very essence of life itself—the Son of God.

Mary was not forced into this role. Willingly, she accepted her mission by telling the angel to let the Word become flesh in her womb. Instead of eating forbidden fruit, she ate obedient fruit, and that made all the difference.

Those chosen today have the water of baptism poured over them after they reject the empty promises of the tricking serpent. They, like Mary, become instruments for God to accomplish his will, and they praise his immaculate glory at work in all who obey. ✠

Meditation

What works has God accomplished through you?

Prayer

We sing you a new song, Lord God, for you have done marvelous deeds through the Blessed Virgin Mary. Heal us with your grace and save our fallen race through Jesus Christ, your Son, whose coming in glory we await. With the Holy Spirit, you are one God, forever and ever. Amen.

Section II:
Second Week of Advent

Second Sunday of Advent, *Cycle A*

Scriptures: Isaiah 11:1–10; Romans 15:4–9; Matthew 3:1–12

Hymn

Isaiah 'twas foretold it,
This Rose I have in mind,
With Mary we behold it,
The Virgin Mother kind.
To show God's love a right,
She bore to us a Savior,
When half spent was the night.

"Lo, How a Rose E'er Blooming," verse 2

Reflection

John the Baptist is the prophet who prepares the way for Jesus with fiery homilies about repentance. Like a lone voice in the middle of the desert that few are able to hear, John challenges religious authorities to demonstrate that they have changed their ways; otherwise, like nonproducing fruit trees, they will be cut down. The One who breaks the fetters of sin will separate the wheat from the chaff in preparation for the arrival of his Father's kingdom.

The One who is coming is Isaiah's shoot from Jesse's stump that has blossomed from the Virgin Mary's womb. He will display God's love not in a culturally sappy manner of hugs and kisses, but with a peace and knowledge of the Lord that brings no harm or ruin on God's holy mountain.

In this new world, the way of life will be different. The wolf will no longer appear in sheep's clothing to trick the lamb. The lion will no longer stalk the calf. Bears and cows will live as next-door neighbors in peace. The man who will reign will be guided by the Lord's Spirit, filled with wisdom, understanding, counsel, strength, knowledge, and awe. When he separates chaff from wheat, his guide will be justice, that is, what is due others in faithfulness. In this new kingdom, both Jews and Gentiles who repent will be welcomed. ✛

Meditation

Of what do you need to repent to share now in the new life of God's kingdom?

Prayer

We glorify you, O God, for the dawn of grace that you have given all people through your Son, Jesus Christ. Through our repentance, intensify our hope of sharing in the kingdom, where you live and reign as one God, forever and ever. Amen.

Second Sunday of Advent, *Cycle B*

Scriptures: Isaiah 40:1–5, 9–11; 1 Peter 3:8–14;
Mark 1:1–8

◇◇

Hymn

The first Nowell, the angel did say,
Was to certain poor shepherds in fields as they lay;
In fields where they lay keeping their sheep,
On a cold winter's night that was so deep.
Nowell, Nowell, Nowell, Nowell,
Born is the King of Israel.

"The First Nowell," verse 1

Reflection

Waiting in line for a table in a restaurant, waiting in line to transact business in a bank, waiting in traffic to get through a light—all make us impatient because we are in a hurry to get somewhere, and we don't want to be delayed. The First Letter of Peter knows that waiting one day for Christ's return in glory is like spending a thousand earth years, because a thousand years to God are like one day. Thus, we should have the same patience as God and wait for new heavens and a new earth.

Yes, the Lord is coming. Isaiah offers comfort to those who have lost patience. Climb a hill and see that the Lord is on his way bounding over desert highways and leveled mountains and smooth plains. "Like a shepherd God feeds his flock and gathers the lambs in his arms" (Isaiah 40:11), just like those poor shepherds were keeping their sheep in the fields when the Lord's angel announced the birth of the

30

King of Israel. The Lord comes with power to dissolve all that was—maybe in flames—and to create something new for those who repent in the waters of the Jordan River at John the Baptist's hand. The Lord comes to comfort his people, like a shepherd "carries the lambs in his bosom and leads the ewes with care" (Isaiah 40:11). By patiently "Adventing" we grow in holiness and devotion and prepare in ourselves a path for Christ's salvation, which begins with baptism in water and the Holy Spirit. ✠

Meditation

What causes you to be impatient during Advent?

Prayer

You come to save your people, O God. Strengthen our patience during your delay, and grant us the grace of repentance as we construct a highway for your Son, our Lord Jesus Christ, who lives and reigns with you and the Holy Spirit, forever and ever. Amen.

Second Sunday of Advent, *Cycle C*

Scriptures: Baruch 5:1–9; Philippians 1:4–6, 8–11; Luke 3:1–6

Hymn

Born thy people to deliver,
Born a child and yet a king,
Born to reign in us forever,
Now thy gracious kingdom bring.
By thine own eternal Spirit
Rule in all our hearts a lone,
By thine all sufficient merit
Raise us to thy glorious throne.

"Come, Thou Long Expected Jesus," verse 2

Reflection

Verse 2 of "Come, Thou Long Expected Jesus" asks Jesus to raise all to his glorious throne, while the Scripture texts portray that glory coming to people on earth. The prophet Baruch instructs Jerusalem to get dressed in the splendor of glory from God, and the Lord will show her glory to all the earth. Those Jews who went into captivity will form such a glorious procession to the holy city that mountains will be made low and gorges will be filled to level ground so that the Jews may advance secure in the glory of God.

The child whose birth all prepare to celebrate established a new Jerusalem, the eternal kingdom of God, through his suffering, death on a cross, and resurrection. As king, he was heralded by John, the son of Zechariah, who prepared the way for this manifestation of God's glory in the same way as had Baruch before him—leveling mountains and filling in gorges.

In this day and time, God's eternal Spirit works in all who await the fullness of the kingdom. On the day of Christ's return, all who have found the Lord ruling in their hearts will be filled with righteousness, that is, a healthy relationship with God that praises God's glory. They will be raised to Christ's glorious throne, where God will be all in all.

In the meantime, God's glory shines in the sunrise and sunset, in the gentle lap of the ocean on the shore, in the bright blue sky, in the branches of the barren tree, in the sleeping earth, in those who gather at your table. If we stop and open our eyes, we will be blinded by the glory of God. ✚

Meditation

Where do you see God's glory revealed?

Prayer

Christ Jesus, through your suffering and death, you have delivered us and established your kingdom among us. Reign in our hearts through the Holy Spirit, that we may found worthy to praise God before his glorious throne when you come in glory. You are Lord, forever and ever. Amen.

Monday of the Second Week of Advent

Scriptures: Isaiah 35:1–10; Luke 5:17–26

Hymn

Daughter of Zion, rise
To greet your infant king;
Nor let your stubborn heart despise
The pardon he will bring.

"The Coming of Our God," verse 3

Reflection

The Bible calls a stubborn heart a hardened heart. In Luke's Gospel, the Pharisees and teachers of the Law are characterized as having hardened hearts. After Jesus pardons a paralyzed man, they want to know why he speaks blasphemy, that is, why he claims to be God, because only God can forgive sins. Jesus knows what they are thinking in their hard hearts, so he tells the paralyzed man to pick up his stretcher and go home.

From an Isaiahian point of view, Jesus is the manifestation of the glory of God. He strengthens feeble hands and weak knees. He is God, who has come to save his people and before whom the lame leap for joy and whose tongue glorifies God. Like the paralyzed man standing up to greet Jesus, during Advent we prepare to greet Christ coming in glory.

All children of God are cautioned to avoid stubborn hearts, the inability to change, blindness that keeps them from seeing God's new works, deafness that keeps them from hearing God's new words. The men bearing the paralyzed man on the stretcher were openhearted, so much so that they scattered the roof tiles and lowered the man into the middle of the house in front of Jesus. They saw incredible things because their hearts were not hardened. God's redeemed, God's openhearted, make their journey entering Zion singing, rising to meet their coming king. ✠

Meditation

What indicates that you are an openhearted person? What indicates that you are a hard-hearted person?

Prayer

O God, you came to save your people in the person of an infant king. Remove all of our hardheartedness, that we may be ready when your Son, Jesus Christ, comes in glory. He is Lord forever and ever. Amen.

Tuesday of the Second Week of Advent

Scriptures: Isaiah 40:1–11; Matthew 18:12–14

Hymn

Go, tell it on the mountain,
Over the hills and ev'rywhere;
Go, tell it on the mountain
That Jesus Christ is born.
The shepherds feared and trembled
When high above the earth
Rang out the angel chorus
That hailed our Savior's birth.

"Go, Tell It on the Mountain," verse 2

Reflection

The prophet Isaiah is a herald's voice. His words are used by John the Baptist to prepare the way of the Lord. Isaiah's exhortation for Zion to be the herald of glad tidings, announcing the arrival of the Lord God with power, is found in "Go, Tell It on the Mountain" as "Go, tell it on the mountain, Over the hills and ev'rywhere."

Isaiah describes God as a shepherd, who feeds his valuable flock, who gathers the lambs in his arms, caressing them against his chest, while leading their mothers, the ewes, with extreme care. Jesus narrates a tale about a shepherd with 100 sheep in the hills, and one wanders away. The shepherd leaves the ninety-nine and searches for the stray until he finds it, rejoicing more over his find than over those who did not wander. Like Isaiah before him, Jesus declares God to be like the shepherd.

God's angel announces the birth of Jesus to shepherds, who are keeping watch over their sheep by night. Even while they tremble with fear, they bow down in prayer. Then, they go see the comfort that God has sent to his people: Jesus Christ.

The herald's voice comforts God's people. The herald's voice calls the people home. The herald's voice reminds all that God's word is trustworthy. The herald's voice prepares the way of the Lord Jesus' return in glory, shouting that he is near. The herald's voice awakens those dreaming in night's darkness, so that they become children of the day and bask in the holy light. ✤

~~~~~~

Meditation

What do you hear the herald's voice saying to you?

~~~~~~

Prayer

Lord Jesus our King, we hear the herald's voice announcing your coming in glory. Prepare us during this Advent season, that we may be gathered into your Father's flock, where you live and reign with the Holy Spirit, one God, forever and ever. Amen.

Wednesday of the Second Week of Advent

Scriptures: Isaiah 40:25–31; Matthew 11:28–30

Hymn

True God of true God,
Light of Light eternal,
Lo, He abhors not the Virgin's womb;
Son of the Father, begotten not created:
O come, let us adore Him,
O come, let us adore Him,
O come, let us adore Him,
Christ the Lord!

"O Come, All Ye Faithful," verse 2

Reflection

There is something about a human God that we don't like; maybe it is that he looks too much like us, especially when we see him as a babe in a cradle after emerging from the Virgin's womb. In fact, being clothed in human weakness, while it discloses the Son's divinity—true God of true God—demeans the Godhead in some way. Maybe that is human pride and arrogance talking!

As Isaiah makes clear, we are not equal to the Holy One. We cannot create out of nothing. The Son was begotten, not created. We faint and grow weary. Our knowledge is always lacking. Our weakness as humans is the occasion for Jesus to offer rest if we accept his easy and light yoke.

Because we are humanly weak, the Holy One finds a remedy in his Son's humanity and provides a model for the rest of us. For those attuned to God's ways, strength replaces weakness as they run the race of life. We look to the One coming from the Light. Even the peaks and valleys spread the rumor that the Lord is coming.

With eagle's wings God makes those in harmony with his ways soar through human death to eternal life. What the Holy One did for his only begotten Son, he promises to do for all who see their humanity as a window for divinity to shine through. In other words, human weakness becomes the recipient of God's holiness. Come, let us adore him. ✤

Meditation

In what ways is your human weakness a means for God to reveal divine power?

Prayer

Come to the earth, Divine Messiah. Return in peace and meekness and clothe our human weakness in your divinity. We await the day when we shall see your face and find eternal rest. You live and reign with the Father and the Holy Spirit, forever and ever. Amen.

Thursday of the Second Week of Advent

Scriptures: Isaiah 41:13–20; Matthew 11:11–15

Hymn

Then cleansed be ev'ry heart from sin,
Make straight the way for God within,
And let each heart prepare a home
Where such a mighty guest may come.
"On Jordan's Bank the Baptist's Cry," verse 2

Reflection

In Matthew's Gospel, Jesus makes clear to the crowds that John the Baptist was Elijah, the one expected by the prophet Malachi to prepare the way of the Lord. Because of his role, John the Baptist is the greatest of those born of women, yet the least in God's kingdom is greater than he. In God's reign, those who are not important on earth take on greater significance. If John the Baptist is Elijah, then Jesus is God, who, like a guest, seeks a home in every heart.

Like John the Baptist being Elijah, we need to be light along the way to make straight the path for God to enter others' lives. Being the light of Christ means serving the poor, addressing injustice, seeking peace. In other words, we both bear the light of Christ to others and we show them the way.

Through our ministry, God demonstrates his care for the afflicted and the needy. Cleansed from sin through the death and resurrection of Christ, we prepare a straight way for God to work within us. On our baptismal day we were given a candle to keep burning until the day of the Lord.

This is the task for us today: to be other John the Baptists, burning candles, displaying God's light, Jesus Christ, to the world. ✤

~~~~~~

Meditation

How are you a John the Baptist?

~~~~~~

Prayer

God of light, you are compassionate to all your works. Make us glow with the light and life of your Son, that many may come to know that you have redeemed the world. We ask this through our Lord Jesus Christ, who lives and reigns with you and the Holy Spirit, one God, forever and ever. Amen.

Friday of the Second Week of Advent

Scriptures: Isaiah 48:17–19; Matthew 11:16–19

Hymn

How silently, how silently
The wondrous gift is giv'n!
So God imparts to human hearts
The blessings of His heav'n.
No ear may hear His coming,
But in this world of sin,
Where meek souls will receive Him, still
The dear Christ enters in.

"O Little Town of Bethlehem," verse 3

Reflection

The most famous poem of St. John of the Cross, a sixteenth-century Carmelite mystic, is titled "Dark Night." In this work he reflects on his feelings of God's absence. The dark night of the soul, coming primarily through suffering of some kind, strips the person of everything so that he or she is ready to see God's face, to experience God's light and love.

John taught that by desiring nothing one is open to receiving everything from God. The person waits in silent hope for God, who, as Isaiah says, leads one on the way he or she should go. God fulfills his promises and light shines as bright as the sun and moon together. Hope triumphs. In the words of the hymn, the wondrous gift is given.

During Advent, we hope that the Messiah will hasten to come again in glory to the earth. Jesus compares people to children who cannot make up their minds. John the Baptist appeared as an ascetic, and people thought he was possessed by a demon. Jesus appeared eating and drinking, and people thought he was a glutton and a drunkard. Yet, the dawn of grace appeared even in John the Baptist's beheading and Jesus' crucifixion.

We await the day when Christ will come in glory, when the blessings of God's heaven will be imparted to us. We await the day when hope will be realized and light will shine in triumph in this world of sin. We beg the Messiah to come, to dispel the dark night, to show his face, and to declare the dawn of grace. In other words, we ask that Christ, the Light, enters into our darkness. ✠

Meditation

What has been your dark night? What grace did you receive?

Prayer

O Lord, our Redeemer, see our waiting in silence and send the Messiah to complete the dawn of grace. Wrap us in your love and instill us with hope that will triumph when Christ will come again. He is Lord forever and ever. Amen.

Saturday of the Second Week of Advent

Scriptures: Sirach 48:1–4, 9–11;
Matthew 17:9a, 10–13

Hymn

Great judge of all in that last day,
Be present then with us we pray;
Your scattered people, Lord, unite,
In vict'ry over Satan's might.

"Creator of the Stars of Night," verse 5

Reflection

Elijah's role as prophet is summarized in the passage from the Book of Sirach. In Matthew's Gospel particularly, John the Baptist is portrayed as Elijah returned to herald the day of the Lord. John the Baptist, like Elijah, is a fiery figure whose words in Matthew's Gospel are like a flaming furnace, calling people to repentance in preparation for the kingdom of heaven.

One of Elijah's responsibilities was to reestablish and reunite the tribes of Jacob, which had been scattered and conquered by foreign world powers, before the day of the Lord. John the Baptist's role was to prepare people for the ministry of Jesus of Nazareth and the kingdom of heaven he inaugurated.

Now, awaiting the return of Christ in glory, we seek his presence to overcome evil, Satan's might. Modern people should be filled with Elijah's fire and John's words. An Advent people, a Church focused on Christ's return, should always be in the process of preparing his way through the lifestyle of her members. All flesh will see God's salvation when Christ comes in glory. ✠

Meditation

Specifically, how are you an Advent person?

Prayer

Lord, make us turn to you through the words of Elijah the prophet and John the Baptist. May we see your face and be saved when Jesus Christ, your Son, comes in glory. He lives and reigns with you and the Holy Spirit, one God, forever and ever. Amen.

Feast: Our Lady of Guadalupe

This feast is celebrated every year on December 12,
except when December 12 falls on a Sunday.

Scriptures: Zechariah 2:14–17 or Revelation
11:19a; 12:1–6a, 10ab; Luke 1:26–38 or Luke 1:39–47

Hymn

You came when old world drew towards night,
Appearing not in princely might,
But born of Mary mother mild,
Became the victim undefiled.
                    "Creator of the Stars of Night," verse 3

Reflection

The child born of the Blessed Virgin Mary is God incarnate. Because of this, Mary is described using Hebrew Bible (Old Testament) metaphors. The passage from the prophet Zechariah calls her the daughter of Zion in whom the Lord came to dwell. The Book of Revelation presents her clothed with the sun, standing on the moon, and crowned with stars; she is a sign in the sky.

Luke's Gospel portrays her as a new ark of the covenant, the gold-covered box containing the tablets of the Law, over whom God's Spirit overshadows. Elizabeth, her relative, declares blessed the fruit of her womb, Jesus. Mary is the bearer of God's presence, the Mother of God, Our Lady of Guadalupe, pregnant with the Son of God.

He came when the old world was going deeper and deeper into darkness, but he did not appear with princely power. He had to come as a common man, so that God would know what it was like to be human, to be a creature. In other words, the Creator experienced creaturehood, even being born of a woman, even dying as a victim on a cross.

His birth from the womb of Mary prepares us for his second birth—his coming in glory—at the end of time. During Advent we look back to one and forward to the other. The instrument of the first was the Blessed Virgin Mary, O0.ur Lady of Guadalupe; the instrument of the second will be his divine authority and power bestowed on him by his resurrection from the dead. ✢

Meditation

What is your favorite image or title for the Blessed Virgin Mary?

Prayer

Most High God, you came to dwell on the earth in the Virgin of Nazareth. Pregnant with your Son, she is a sign of your presence with your people. Through the intercession of Our Lady of Guadalupe, prepare us for Christ's return in glory. He is Lord forever and ever. Amen.

Section III:
Third Week of Advent

*Beginning December 17, the Advent weekday readings
are interrupted by reflections on the "O Antiphons."
On this date, regardless of the day of the week it lands,
skip to Section IV to commence these reflections. However,
for the Sunday between December 17 and 25, use the
material from the fourth Sunday of Advent in Section IV.*

Third Sunday of Advent, *Cycle A*

Scriptures: Isaiah 35:1–6a, 10; James 5:7–10;
Matthew 11:2–11

Hymn

O holy Child of Bethlehem,
Descend to us, we pray;
Cast out our sin and enter in,
Be born in us today.
We hear the Christmas angels
The great glad tidings tell;
O come with us, abide with us,
Our Lord, Emmanuel!

"O Little Town of Bethlehem," verse 5

Reflection

The evidence speaks for itself, Jesus tells John the Baptist's disciples. They have heard the rumors and seen Jesus' deeds of restoring sight to the blind, ambulation to the lame, healing to the lepers, hearing to the deaf, and life to the dead. Likewise, James presents as evidence the patience of the farmer awaiting rain and the fruit of his labor. Even though the earth is bare, a seed has been planted. The rain will nourish it and it will flower and flourish. The evidence declares that God has descended in the person of Jesus and saved his people, as Isaiah declared centuries ago.

Once we have the evidence, we must be patient. The coming of Christ is at hand, so we prepare by not complaining. We use as our model the patience of the prophets, who spoke glad tidings in God's name and waited for God to act. The last of these mighty preachers was John the Baptist, declared by Jesus to be the greatest among those born of women. He prepared the way; we prepare a throne. He sang alone in the desert; we sing together in joyful song about the Lord's mighty deeds as we await his descent in glory. One day he will be born in us, come with us, and abide with us forever. ✠

Meditation

What evidence of God's works is presented to you in today's Scripture texts?

Prayer

Lord, as we await the advent of your Son in glory, grant that we may hear deeply the words of your prophets and prepare a throne for him, who lives and reigns with you and the Holy Spirit forever and ever. Amen.

Third Sunday of Advent, *Cycle B*

Scriptures: Isaiah 61:1–2a, 10–11;
1 Thessalonians 5:16–24; John 1:6–8, 19–28

Hymn

Come, Holy Ghost, Creator blest,
And in our hearts take up thy rest;
Come with thy grace and heav'nly aid
To fill the hearts which thou hast made;
To fill the hearts which thou hast made.

"Come, Holy Ghost" verse 1

Reflection

When God pours Spirit on us, that is, when the Lord anoints us with himself, he sends us to others with a radical message. For example, instead of complaints, we bring glad tidings to the poor. Instead of depression, we bring healing to the brokenhearted. To those who are held captive by addiction—to alcohol, drugs, sex, technology—we announce liberty. If people are prisoners to preconceived ideas, we release them. Basically, the Lord God's Spirit sends us to announce that this is a good year.

John the Baptist had the Holy Spirit poured on him, and he went to others to testify to the light of Christ. Even when authorities confronted him, he declared that the Spirit enabled him to deliver his radical message and to enact his radical act of baptism in preparation for one coming after him. While some scorned his message, others heeded it and rejoiced in it.

In the waters of baptism, we have been anointed with the Spirit that enables us to rejoice and pray always, to give thanks to God in all circumstances while we await the coming of our Lord Jesus Christ in glory. Complaints, depression, addictions, and self-imprisonment dampen the Spirit's fire. That's why Paul tells the Thessalonians not to quench the Spirit but stoke the sacred fire and receive the Holy One's inspiration. ✢

Meditation

In what specific ways are you on fire with the Holy Spirit?

Prayer

Holy Spirit, Wisdom of God, pour on us your holy anointing, that we may become perfectly holy and be preserved entirely blameless in soul and body for the coming of our Lord Jesus Christ, who lives and reigns with you and the Father, forever and ever. Amen.

Third Sunday of Advent, *Cycle C*

Scriptures: Zephaniah 3:14–18a; Philippians 4:4–7; Luke 3:10–18

Hymn

On Jordan's bank the Baptist's cry
Announces that the Lord is nigh;
Awake and harken, for he brings
Glad tidings of the King of kings.

"On Jordan's Bank the Baptist's Cry," *verse 1*

Reflection

There is a lot of shouting going on today. The prophet Zephaniah calls on Jerusalem to shout for joy because the Lord, the King of Israel, is in her midst. Likewise, Paul exhorts the Philippians to rejoice because the Lord, Jesus Christ, is near. And Luke's John the Baptist stands on the bank of the Jordan River announcing that God's kingdom is coming.

The proper response to all this crying or shouting or rejoicing when faced with the imminence of God's kingdom is given by John the Baptist. Those with two cloaks need to give one away. Food should be shared. Tax collectors should not take more than what the Roman government has levied. Roman soldiers should be satisfied with their pay and not look for ways to increase it illegally. In other words, when faced with the imminent arrival of God's kingdom, all should awake and harken at these words of good news, these glad tidings that the King of kings is coming.

For hundreds of years, prophets and apostles have tried to awaken people and get them to respond to their words that God is in their midst, that the Lord is near, that someone mightier is coming, that Christ is returning soon, that the kingdom of God is here. Such good news should provoke a response of gratitude, of sharing, of reform of life. Such good news should find its hearers shouting, crying, rejoicing. ✠

Meditation

What response do you make to the words of the prophets and apostles that God's kingdom is here?

Prayer

King of Israel, Lord, you are in our midst; you are near to those who hear the words of your prophets and apostles. Give us the grace to respond to their words, that we may be found worthy to enter your kingdom when Christ comes in glory. He lives and reigns forever and ever. Amen.

Monday of the Third Week of Advent

Scriptures: Numbers 24:2–7, 15–17a; Matthew 21:23–27

Hymn

Songs of thankfulness and praise,
Jesus, Lord, to thee we raise;
Manifested by the star
To the sages from afar,
Branch of royal David's stem
In thy birth at Bethlehem:
Anthems be to thee addressed,
God in flesh made manifest.

"Songs of Thankfulness and Praise," verse 1

Reflection

Balaam was brought by Balak, Israel's enemy, to curse the tribes of Israel. In other words, he was supposed to condemn them to darkness. He was, however, overcome by the spirit of God, and he ended up blessing them. Furthermore, he declares that a star will rise out of the tribe of Jacob, that a staff will rise from Israel. Because this prophecy was written after David united all the tribes into a confederacy and ascended the throne, the starlight reference is to the greatest king of Judah. Later, it was applied to Jesus, a branch from David's royal stem.

In a reversal similar to Balaam's blessing instead of cursing Israel, Jesus is cornered by the religious authorities of his day who want to discredit him. After they ask him the source of his authority, he decides to play their power game by asking them about John the Baptist's baptism. They cannot answer him and win, so he refuses to shine light on their question.

The Scriptures of Advent are filled with riddles of people like Balaam, about whom we may have never heard, and Jesus. When we ponder them, we come to know what the Most High knows and see what the Almighty sees. All we can do is offer songs of thankfulness and praise to God in flesh made manifest, the One who was revealed by a star to those who sought wisdom. And this wisdom is light that illumines our dark nights. ✠

Meditation

What darkness in your life has recently been illumined by God's word?

Prayer

O Lord, you teach us your ways through the light of your word. Quiet our minds that we may hear what you say and know what you know. Open our eyes to see your works and recognize the light of your Son, Jesus Christ, who lives with you in the unity of the Holy Spirit, forever and ever. Amen.

Tuesday of the Third Week of Advent

Scriptures: Zephaniah 3:1–2, 9–13;
Matthew 21:28–32

Hymn

For, lo, the days are hastening on,
By prophet bards foretold,
When with the ever-circling years
Comes 'round the age of gold;
When peace shall over all the earth
Its ancient splendors fling,
And all the world give back the song
Which now the angels sing.

"It Came Upon the Midnight Clear," verse 4

Reflection

Judge, judgment, and judging are not popular words in American culture. Citizens of the United States consider themselves from an independent, individualist perspective, that is, whatever the individual thinks is true. Thus, no one has the right to judge the actions of another. Even in schools, teachers, who used to be responsible for correcting students' behavior and giving grades to indicate the degree of success, are criticized for judging the young men and women sitting in the desks before them.

There is no problem with judge, judgment, and judging in biblical literature, however. The prophet Zephaniah records God's judgment against the rebellious and polluted city of Jerusalem, which, like modern people, hears no voice and accepts no correction. Likewise, Jesus asks religious authorities to judge between a son who first said no to his father but changed his mind and one who said yes but never did his father's will. The first son is compared to tax collectors and prostitutes who are entering God's kingdom before those who judged themselves to be righteous.

God always preserves a remnant, a few people who hear the judgment and change their lives. What does it take for us to accept the judgment that we are wrong and, therefore, in need of reform? The religious authorities of Jesus' day saw tax collectors and prostitutes respond to John the Baptist's judgment and they still did not change their minds.

We are given these hastening-on days as we await Christ's return in glory. He will come as judge and bring peace to those who have followed him sincerely. When that day arrives, we will sing the song the angels chanted at Jesus' birth: Peace on earth and goodwill to all. ✠

Meditation

What judgment do you hear that challenges you to reform your life?

Prayer

Lord, through your prophets you judge your people and call them to reform their lives. As we await the dawning of your Son in glory, forgive our sins and guide our feet in the paths of righteousness. We ask this through our Lord Jesus Christ, who lives and reigns with you in the unity of the Holy Spirit, one God, forever and ever. Amen.

Wednesday of the Third Week of Advent

Scriptures: Isaiah 45:6c–8, 18, 21c–25; Luke 7:18b–23

Hymn

For you are our salvation, Lord,
Our refuge, and our great reward:
Without your grace we waste away,
Like flow'rs that wither and decay.

"On Jordan's Bank the Baptist's Cry," verse 3

Reflection

Through the prophet Isaiah, God reminds us who is in charge. A people who thinks it determines the course of world events is in direct conflict with the Lord, the designer and maker of the earth, the creator of light and darkness, the source of well-being and woe. Jesus tells John the Baptist's two disciples that he is in charge of the blind seeing, the lame walking, the lepers cleansed, the deaf hearing, the dead raised, and the poor lifted up.

Once we know that we are not in charge, then we can beseech the Holy One to let his justice descend like dew from the heavens. God's justice is not American jurisprudence, which is usually characterized as what is fair. The Lord's justice that falls like a gentle rain is what is owed to others. Salvation brings sight, walking, cleansing, hearing, new life, because the Savior re-creates and restores what sin has tarnished. Without this grace, we wither like cut flowers. As the earth brings forth a Savior who showers it with justice, grace, and new life, all we can do is kneel before him and his Father. ✠

Meditation

What has sprung forth in you after you recognized who was in charge?

Prayer

Lord, creator of heaven and earth, you are God, and there is no other. In the fullness of time, your justice descended like dew, like gentle rain the skies dropped it down, and salvation budded forth. As we await the Second Coming of your Son, be our refuge. We ask this in the name of Jesus, who is Lord forever and ever. Amen.

Thursday of the Third Week of Advent

Scriptures: Isaiah 54:1–10; Luke 7:24–30

Hymn

Now let earth and heav'n adore you,
As saints and angels sing before you
With harp and cymbal's joyful tone:
Of one pearl each shining portal,
Where we join with the choirs immortal
Of angels round your dazzling throne.
No eye has seen, nor ear
Is yet attuned to hear
Such great glory,
Alleluia, as we sing
Our praise to you, eternal King!

"Wake, Awake! For Night Is Flying," verse 3

Reflection

Isaiah sings about incredible things: barren women, women deserted by their husbands, children deserted by their fathers. In God's world, all human values—children, marriage, faithfulness—are reversed. The Holy One of Israel will assume the role of husband; he summons the wife he abandoned to the Babylonians, extending his arms in great tenderness to reach out and welcome back her from whom he hid his face. He promises her everlasting love.

The everlasting love of God became incarnate in Jesus of Nazareth, who praised John the Baptist for preparing his way. Like Isaiah before him, Jesus speaks about incredible things: John the Baptist is the greatest of all born of women but the least in God's kingdom.

What attracts us during Advent? Trees swayed by the wind? Fine garments displayed in department store windows? Party tables filled with sumptuous food and fine drinks? Shouldn't the incredible things of God—the Incarnation, salvation, redemption—be our focus? If so, then all we can do is praise the Holy One for such great glory revealed through incredible things. ✢

Meditation

What is the most incredible thing God has done for you?

Prayer

Holy One of Israel, earth and heaven adore you, as saints and angels sing before you. We join with them in praising you for all your incredible works through our Lord Jesus Christ, your Son, who lives and reigns with you and the Holy Spirit, one God, forever and ever. Amen.

Friday of the Third Week of Advent

Scriptures: Isaiah 56:1–3a, 6–8; John 5:33–36

Hymn

The everlasting Son
Was born to make us free;
And he a servant's form put on
To gain our liberty.

"The Coming of Our God," verse 2

Reflection

The salvation that Isaiah announced was near and has come in the person of Jesus Christ. This liberty was achieved by the Lord for all people—Jews and Gentiles, whom Isaiah refers to as foreigners. In John's Gospel, after declaring John the Baptist a burning and shining lamp, Jesus trumps John's light with his declaration that the Father sent him with works to accomplish.

That primary work was to unite humanity by making God's temple a house of prayer for all people. Gentiles who believed in the Lord and loved his name and honored him on the day he reserved for himself joined to Jews, the children of Abraham, to form a single assembly of prayer by Jesus. He, the everlasting Son, was born to set all free from everything that could possibly divide them.

Cultural individuality in its most extreme form is based on differences, what distinguishes, what separates people one from another, one group from another, one church from another, one religion from another. The work that God sent Jesus to accomplish is not yet finished.

Those who prepare for his coming in glory during Advent recognize that they have been handed the torch and must now spread the light. ✠

Meditation

What work of unity has been entrusted to you?

Prayer

Lord God, you made John the Baptist a burning and shining lamp to show your people the way to you. You increased John's light and gave even greater works to your everlasting Son, who testified that you desire one house of prayer in which all can praise your Son. Guide us to deeper unity through the Holy Spirit, who lives and reigns with you and our Lord Jesus Christ, one God, forever and ever. Amen.

Section IV:
Fourth Week
and Late Advent Weekdays

This section includes the reflections on the "O Antiphons."

Fourth Sunday of Advent, *Cycle A*

Scriptures: Isaiah 7:10–14; Romans 1:1–7; Matthew 1:18–24

Hymn

O Flow'r, whose fragrance tender
With sweetness fills the air,
Dispel in glorious splendor
The darkness of ev'ry where;
True man, yet very God,
From sin and death now save us,
And share our ev'ry load.

"Lo, How a Rose E'er Blooming," verse 3

Reflection

In the opening of his Letter to the Romans, Paul summarizes the other two biblical texts assigned for this fourth Sunday of Advent. He declares that God's Son was descended from David according to the flesh, but established as Son of God in power according to the Spirit of holiness through resurrection from the dead. After presenting an extensive genealogy, Matthew declares that Joseph is a descendant of David. As foster father of Mary's child, that makes the One conceived in her womb by the Holy Spirit a descendant of David, too. Isaiah had long ago told King Ahaz, a descendant of David, that the Lord would give him a sign of a son, who would be called Emmanuel, to indicate that God was with his people in Judah during the time of crisis in which Ahaz was king. Matthew stretches this prophecy to apply it to Jesus, the incarnate presence of God, indeed the literal presence of God with people, true man yet true God.

The third verse of "Lo, How a Rose E'er Blooming" also captures the essence of today's Scripture texts. Jesus is the rose, whose fragrance fills the air with sweetness. He is the Savior of the world, the one who frees all from sin and death. Isaiah prophesied his coming. The Virgin of Nazareth conceived him. Joseph dreamed about him. And Paul put into words his gospel of obedient faith. As we take our attention off of his coming in glory and focus on preparing to celebrate his birth in human history, we should lift our heads and, like gates, open our minds to the glory of the Flower of Jesse's stem, Jesus Christ. ✤

Meditation

In what specific ways are you preparing to celebrate the birth of Jesus Christ?

Prayer

The earth and its fullness and the world belong to you, O Lord. With the birth of your Son, Emmanuel, your glory was manifest in human nature. Grant to us the obedience of faith, that we may be counted among all others who belong to Jesus Christ, who is Lord forever and ever. Amen.

Fourth Sunday of Advent, *Cycle B*

Scriptures: 2 Samuel 7:1–5, 8b–12, 14a, 16;
Romans 16:25–27; Luke 1:26–38

Hymn

Silent night, holy night!
All is calm, all is bright.
Round yon Virgin Mother and Child.
Holy Infant so tender and mild,
Sleep in heavenly peace,
Sleep in heavenly peace.

"Silent Night," verse 1

Reflection

We call them secrets; Paul calls them mysteries. Nathan, one of King David's prophets, calls them double entendres, words that can have more than one meaning in context. They are things we think we know, but it is only surface knowledge, that is, we know only about them. Once we plumb the depths of secrets and mysteries and double entendres, we actually know them; we glean the wisdom of God.

For Paul the mystery kept secret for many ages is that God chooses all people through the death and resurrection of his Son. For Nathan the mystery is that God is not interested in David building a house for him; instead, the Lord will construct a house for David, a happy home. Heirs of David will occupy his house and sit on his throne forever. Luke makes us aware that Joseph, Mary's betrothed, is of the house of David. Through the Virgin, God will keep his promise to David by favoring this young woman with grace, pouring on her the Holy Spirit, and overshadowing her with the Most High's own power.

For us the mystery is that God has blessed our land, our cities, our homes, our hearts through the Incarnation and birth of his Son. As we complete our Advent preparation and get ready to mark the silent, holy night, we realize that we can only sing of the Lord's goodness. And that awareness is true wisdom that leads to heavenly peace. ✠

Meditation

What secret, mystery, or double entendre has God revealed to you?

Prayer

Most High God, you have confirmed your faithfulness to your covenant through the birth of your Son, our Lord Jesus Christ. As we prepare to celebrate his Nativity, fill us with your Spirit of wisdom. To you, the only wise God, through Jesus Christ, be glory forever and ever. Amen.

Fourth Sunday of Advent, *Cycle C*

Scriptures: Micah 5:1–4a, Hebrews 10:5–10; Luke 1:39–45

Hymn

The coming of our God
Our thoughts must now employ;
Then let us meet him on the road
With songs of holy joy.

"The Coming of Our God," verse 1

Reflection

Bethlehem-Ephrathah, mentioned by the prophet Micah, is the hometown of David, the king of Israel. From this village, which needs two names to be recognized, comes forth one whose greatness reached the ends of the earth. In Luke's Gospel, Mary comes to Elizabeth in an unnamed village. The mother of the Lord brings him in her womb to meet the child in Elizabeth's womb, John the Baptist, who leaps for joy.

The reflections of the author of Hebrews remind the reader that God did not desire holocausts and sin offerings, but he wanted his creation to do his will. And that is what Jesus, for whom he prepared a body in the womb of the Virgin, did: Christ did the will of God.

Today, the thoughts of all turn to the Nativity, the coming of God in the person of Jesus. The end of the Advent road is in sight, and songs of holy joy, like that voiced by Elizabeth after Mary came to her, should be on our lips. Christ should be greeted with sacred hymns—not the secular tunes about Santa Claus and Rudolph that clog the airways. ✢

Meditation

What sacred carols are your singing to welcome the coming Nativity?

Prayer

Lord, Father of our Lord Jesus Christ, you came to us as creator and savior, as shepherd and redeemer, in the flesh of your Son and in the power of your Spirit. As we prepare to celebrate the Nativity of Jesus, come to us with inspiration from the Spirit that we may praise you and them as one God, forever and ever. Amen.

December 17

Hymn

O come, thou wisdom from on high,
And order all things far and nigh;
To us the path of knowledge show,
And teach us in her ways to go.
Rejoice! Rejoice!
Emmanuel shall come to thee, O Israel.
"O Come, O Come, Emmanuel," verse 2

Reflection

A biblical presupposition is that God created the world and owns it. One of God's attributes as creator is wisdom, which guides and informs his creative power and can impart knowledge to those who study his works. The second verse of "O Come, O Come, Emmanuel" begs for this wisdom from on high to reorder the chaos caused by sin and reveal and teach to all the path of knowledge, the path of wisdom.

God's wisdom is seen in Jacob's words to his sons before he dies about the tribe of Judah becoming greater than the other tribes. Judah is compared to a lion. Disclosing the fact that this passage was written after Judah became the southern Kingdom, Jacob's words remind the reader that the scepter, the king, shall never depart from Judah.

The author of Matthew's Gospel sees God's wisdom traced through Jesus' genealogy, not only because it mentions Judah but because its neatly arranged three sets of fourteen names is also the numerical value of the

Hebrew letters that spell David. Even though there are not fourteen names in each set, Matthew's point remains: God's wisdom guides his creation through the patriarchs, the kings, the Babylonian captivity, and many unknown people of the past and leads to the rejoicing that should occur as Emmanuel comes onto the scene.

A turning point occurs in Advent preparation today. The past weeks have been focused on Christ's return in glory. For the next eight days, the focus shifts to immediate preparation to celebrate Jesus' birth, or Nativity. ✠

Meditation

In what specific ways do you experience God's wisdom in your life?

Prayer

O Wisdom of God Most High, who guides creation with power and love, come to teach us the path of knowledge, that we may recognize your saving deeds among us. Hear us through our Lord Jesus Christ, your Son, for whose Nativity we prepare to celebrate. He lives and reigns with you and the Holy Spirit, one God, forever and ever. Amen.

December 18

Scriptures: Jeremiah 23:5–8; Matthew 1:18–25

Hymn

O come, thou holy Lord of might,
Who to thy tribes on Sinai's height
In ancient times did give the law,
In cloud and majesty and awe.
Rejoice! Rejoice!
Emmanuel shall come to thee, O Israel.
"O Come, O Come, Emmanuel," verse 3

Reflection

Jeremiah, living after the destruction of Jerusalem and the Temple by the Babylonians, hears the Lord declare that one day he will raise up a righteous shoot to David, that is, a Davidic descendant, who will gather his people from the land of the north, Babylon, and bring them back to Israel.

Before Jeremiah, this holy Lord of might gave his Law, or Torah, to the twelve tribes of Israel through Moses, who received the tablets in cloud and majesty and awe on Mount Sinai. Jeremiah's righteous shoot to David will be named justice; his relationship with God will be in right order, and he will give others what is due them, governing wisely.

The author of Matthew's Gospel understands Jesus to be David's descendant, because Joseph, his foster father, is a son of David, and because he is known as Emmanuel, which means that God is with his people. Jesus will preach a new righteousness and call people to practice justice—to put others ahead of themselves in terms of what is owed to them. Jesus' new righteousness will also serve as a new law, or Torah, that exhorts people to do the right thing because it is the right thing to do. It is summarized by loving God, loving neighbor, and loving self selflessly. ✛

Meditation

How do you practice the new righteousness?

Prayer

Lord God, leader of all, giver of the Law to Moses on Mount Sinai, we rejoice that you have rescued us with the mighty power of Emmanuel. Make us righteous and keep us faithful to our Lord Jesus Christ, your Son, who lives and reigns with you and the Holy Spirit, one God, forever and ever. Amen.

December 19

Hymn

O come, thou rod of Jesse's stem,
From ev'ry foe deliver them.
From death and sin thy people save,
And give them vict'ry o'er the grave.
Rejoice! Rejoice!
Emmanuel shall come to thee, O Israel.

"O Come, O Come, Emmanuel," *verse 4*

Reflection

In many Gothic cathedrals there is a stained-glass window dedicated to Jesse, the father of King David. Jesse is shown in the lowest panel with a shoot or small tree growing out of his stomach. On the upward twisting branches in the panes above are perched various kings of Judah. On the top of the tree sits the Blessed Virgin Mary holding the baby Jesus, who is the rod of Jesse's stem, who comes to deliver people from death and sin and give them new life through his own resurrection from the grave.

The birth of Emmanuel, the death- and sin-deliverer, is preceded by the birth of another deliverer in the Book of Judges. Manoah and his wife are barren. An angel appears to this unnamed woman and tells her that she will conceive a son, who will deliver his people from their enemies. Samson is to be consecrated to God from the womb. When the Spirit of God stirred him, Samson became a judge and a leader of his people, and he died delivering them from their enemies.

The announcement of the conception and birth of Luke's John the Baptist is modeled on the Samson story. Elizabeth is barren, but Zechariah entertains the angel Gabriel, who tells him that Elizabeth will conceive, the child will be dedicated to God, and that the Holy Spirit will fill him in his mother's womb. He will prepare the way for the Messiah, the root of Jesse's stem. ✠

Meditation

Out of what barrenness in your life has God brought forth new life?

Prayer

O root of Jesse's stem, you are the sign of God's love for his people. Come in glory to save the people you have redeemed through your suffering and death. By the power of your resurrection, give us victory over the grave. You are Lord forever and ever. Amen.

December 20

Scriptures: Isaiah 7:10–14; Luke 1:26–38

Hymn

O come, thou key of David, come,
And open wide our heav'nly home,
Make safe the way that leads on high,
And close the path to misery.
Rejoice! Rejoice!
Emmanuel shall come to thee, O Israel.
"O Come, O Come, Emmanuel," verse 5

Reflection

Most people carry a ring with a number of keys on it. Usually among the collection is a house key, a car key, an office key, a safe deposit box key, and many others. In some instances, a desk key opens the drawer that contains more keys to file cabinets, closets, and supply bins. Jesus is the key of David, who opened the gates of heaven, made safe the way to God's kingdom, and locked the path to misery.

Through Isaiah, God spoke to King Ahaz, as he was under siege by his enemies. The Lord gave him, a descendant of David, a key, a sign; a young woman would conceive and bear a son. The son would be named Emmanuel, which means that God is with his people. In other words, Ahaz is assured that he will have a descendant who will sit on his throne, and that son-descendant will be the presence of God on the throne of Judah. So, Ahaz rejoiced that Emmanuel would come to him.

The angel Gabriel gives a key to the Virgin of Nazareth, the woman betrothed to Joseph of the house of David. Mary is told that if she will cooperate, God's key, the Holy Spirit, will conceive in her womb a child, who will be called the Son of God. He will sit on David's throne, and his kingdom will be without end. Jesus will be not just a sign of God's presence with his people, but he will be God incarnate with his people. So Mary rejoices that Emmanuel came to her and to all Israel. ✠

Meditation

What key has God used to open you to Emmanuel?

Prayer

Lord Jesus Christ, Key of David, through your death and resurrection, you opened the gates of God's eternal kingdom. Make safe the way for us prisoners of this world's darkness, that we may one day rejoice with you in heaven, where you live and reign with the Father and the Holy Spirit, one God, forever and ever. Amen.

December 21

Scriptures: Song of Songs 2:8–14 or
Zephaniah 3:14–18a, Luke 1:39–45

Hymn

O come, thou dayspring, come and cheer
Our spirits by thine advent here;
Disperse the gloomy clouds of night
And death's dark shadow put to flight.
Rejoice! Rejoice!
Emmanuel shall come to thee, O Israel.

"O Come, O Come, Emmanuel," verse 6

Reflection

A visit happens when one person spends time with another. One friend goes to dinner in the home of another friend; one has visited the other. During holidays, people travel across the country to visit family members who live considerable distances apart. Recognizing someone on the street and stopping and talking with him or her is a visit.

In the poetic passage from the Song of Songs, the lover visits his beloved. While walking through the mountains, he sings and leaps for joy at the prospect of seeing the woman he loves. The prophet Zephaniah declares that God is visiting his people; God, a mighty savior, is in the midst of Jerusalem. And the author of Luke's Gospel uniquely narrates the account of Mary visiting Elizabeth, whose child leapt in her womb for joy when Elizabeth heard Mary's voice of greeting at the front door.

In the sixth verse from "O Come, O Come, Emmanuel," the advent of the first light of day, the dayspring, cheers the spirits of those waiting for the sunrise. The dawn visitor disperses the gloom of night; it scatters death's dark shadow. In other words, the visit of Jesus, Emmanuel, to the world was light that sent darkness fleeing. And in his light, the world rejoices. ✠

Meditation

What affect do the first streaks of dawn have on your spirit?

Prayer

Lord Jesus Christ, you are the dayspring from on high who has cheered us and caused us to rejoice greatly at your Nativity. As we prepare to celebrate your birth, disperse the gloom of sin. Through your death and resurrection you have destroyed the power of death. You live and reign with the Father and the Holy Spirit, forever and ever. Amen.

December 22

Hymn

O come, desire of nations, bind
In one the hearts of humankind;
Bid ev'ry sad division cease
And be thyself our Prince of peace.
Rejoice! Rejoice!
Emmanuel shall come to thee, O Israel.
                    "O Come, O Come, Emmanuel," verse 7

Reflection

Modern people, just like ancient ones, divide themselves in all kinds of ways. They are, for example, male or female, Democrat or Republican, white or black with every shade in between, homeowners or apartment renters, and Catholic or Protestant. It seems that identity is achieved at the price of division.

Hannah, mother of Samuel, gives birth to the judge, prophet, priest, and king-maker who will attempt to end the divisions of his people. Samuel anoints Saul as king in an attempt to bring together the tribes of Israel. When that fails, he anoints David, who successfully unites the tribes into a nation, which lasts through his reign and that of his son, Solomon.

Mary's song, as recorded in Luke's Gospel, is about God uniting his people by leveling self-importance, by instituting egalitarianism. The Virgin of Nazareth gives voice to the deepest desire of people of all nations, namely, that God bind into one the hearts of all humankind so that the sad divisions cease and peace rules the world. The Virgin's son, the Prince of Peace, left that task to all who follow him. ✢

Meditation

In what ways do you unite others rather than divide them during Advent?

Prayer

Lord Jesus Christ, King of all nations, keystone of the Catholic Church, bind in one the hearts of your people so that their sad divisions cease. Prince of Peace, prepare us to celebrate your Nativity. You live and reign with the Father and the Holy Spirit, one God, forever and ever. Amen.

December 23

Scriptures: Malachi 3:1–4, 23–24; Luke 1:57–66

Hymn

In glory from His throne
Again will Christ descend,
And summon all that are His own
To joys that never end.

"The Coming of Our God," verse 4

Reflection

The fourth verse of "The Coming of Our God" aptly summarizes today's Scripture texts. The prophet Malachi declares that the fiery Lord God, the sovereign of the world, is coming from his heavenly throne to his earthly temple. Before that great and terrible day, the prophet Elijah, who was taken to heaven in a fiery chariot, will appear to prepare for God's arrival.

A new and nobler life begins in Luke's Gospel. The Holy Spirit has been guiding the events of Zechariah and Elizabeth and Mary and Joseph. Now, Zechariah's and Elizabeth's son is born and named John the Baptist. Even the hill folk recognize that God's hand is on this new child, who has appeared to prepare for the arrival of Jesus.

These last days of Advent are given to us to prepare for the arrival of family and friends to our home. We don't want to be so caught up in their coming, however, that we forget whose arrival we really celebrate: Jesus Christ. Malachi knows God is coming. Zechariah and Elizabeth know Jesus is coming. Even in the womb John the Baptist knew that God was coming in the child Mary carried in her womb. We know that Christ will descend from his throne one day and gather all his own to share everlasting joy. John leapt for joy, and so should we as the day of Jesus' Nativity draws near. ✠

Meditation

Who is arriving in your life, in your house?

Prayer

Our God, our rock, our savior, we sing of your goodness as we prepare to celebrate the Nativity of your Son. Grant us the grace of preparedness that we may welcome him with joy. He lives and reigns with you and the Holy Spirit, one God, forever and ever. Amen.

December 24

Scriptures: 2 Samuel 7:1–5, 8b–12, 14a, 16;
Luke 1:67–79

Hymn

O come, O come, Emmanuel,
And ransom captive Israel,
That mourns in lonely exile here
Until the Son of God appear.
Rejoice! Rejoice!
Emmanuel shall come to thee, O Israel.

"O Come, O Come, Emmanuel," verse 1

Reflection

The author of Luke's Gospel portrays Zechariah, the father of John the Baptist, as blessing the God of Israel for having raised up a mighty Savior, born of the house of his servant David. This one fulfills God's promise made to Abraham, namely, that he would set free his people to worship him in holiness and righteousness all the days of their lives.

The mighty Savior born of David's house, about which Zechariah sings, reminds the reader of God's words to King David through Nathan his prophet. When David wanted to build a house for the ark of the covenant—because it was living in a tent—God revealed that he would build a house for David, a dynasty that would last forever. Just as David had been like a son to God, so would the Lord be a father to David's descendants and they like sons to him.

The prophet of the Most High who prepared the way for the last Davidic heir was John the Baptist, sung about by Zechariah, his father. John preached salvation by the forgiveness of sins through baptism in the Jordan River. Jesus, Emmanuel, the Son of God, appeared and ransomed his people who were exiled on earth. To save means to heal; Jesus healed the broken relationship between the Father and his children and initiated the kingdom of God. ✛

Meditation

In what ways has the mighty Savior healed your broken relationship with God?

Prayer

Lord Jesus Christ, Emmanuel, like the breaking dawn you shine upon all who dwell in darkness and the shadow of death. As we prepare to celebrate your Nativity, guide our feet into the way of your peace. You live and reign with the Father and the Holy Spirit, one God, forever and ever. Amen.

Section V:
Solemnity and Octave
of Christmas

The Christmas season ends with the Baptism of the Lord, which doubly serves as the beginning of Ordinary Time. Epiphany is not the end of the Christmas season. The practice of "twelve days of Christmas" was removed by the reforms coming out of Vatican II with the publication of the new liturgical calendar in 1969.

December 25: The Nativity of the Lord

Scriptures:
- *Vigil:* Isaiah 62:1–5; Acts 13:16–17, 22–25;
  Matthew 1:1–25 or 1:18–25
- *Night:* Isaiah 9:1–6; Titus 2:11–14; Luke 2:1–14
- *Dawn:* Isaiah 62:11–12; Titus 3:4–7; Luke 2:15–20
- *Day:* Isaiah 52:7–10; Hebrews 1:1–6; John 1:1–18

Hymn

O come, all ye faithful, joyful and triumphant,
O come ye, O come ye to Bethlehem;
Come and behold Him born the king of angels:
O come, let us adore Him, O come, let us adore
* Him,*
O come, let us adore Him, Christ the Lord!

"O Come, All Ye Faithful," verse 1

Reflection

No matter which set of Scriptures are read on this Solemnity of the Nativity of the Lord, the theme is presence. God is present in Jerusalem, declares the prophet Isaiah, calling the city his delight, his fiancée, the place he frequents. God is present through the narrative of Jesus' genealogy to Abraham and David, accomplishing his will through some of the most unlikely of ancestors.

God is present in David's birthplace, Bethlehem, as Mary gives birth to her Son, Jesus. Angels announce God's presence in the person of a Child to shepherds, who go to see what has taken place. This Child is the Incarnation of the Word of God, who was with God in the beginning and now is God in human flesh, seeking to know what it is like to be a creature.

The hymn "O Come, All Ye Faithful" is the appropriate response before such an awesome mystery. Repeatedly, all believers are called to recognize the presence of God and adore the king of angels, Christ the Lord, just like the angels and shepherds do in the Scripture texts. In times past, God made his presence known through his prophets, but now he has revealed himself in a Son. ✢

Meditation

What makes you aware of God's presence?

Prayer

O Lord, you have revealed your presence to your people and made your salvation known through the Incarnation and Nativity of your Son, Jesus Christ. Grant us the grace to sing your praises and adore him, who lives and reigns with you and the Holy Spirit, one God, forever and ever. Amen.

December 26: St. Stephen

Scriptures: Acts 6:8–10; 7:54–59; Matthew 10:17–22

Hymn

Good King Wenceslas looked out
On the feast of Stephen.
When the snow lay round about
Deep and crisp and even.
Brightly shone the moon that night
Though the frost was cruel.
When a poor man came in sight
Gath'ring winter fuel.

"Good King Wenceslas," verse 1

Reflection

"Good King Wenceslas" is a unique Christmas carol because it does not mention the Nativity. Wenceslas was king of Bohemia in the tenth century and was martyred for his faith. The hymn is a ballad, depicting King Wenceslas seeing a poor man gathering wood on the day after Christmas, the feast of St. Stephen, the first Christian martyr, and deciding to invite him to food and drink and fire in the palace. In the carol, the king tells his page that blessings come to those who help the poor.

The Scripture texts for the feast of St. Stephen announce the same truth. Stephen is one of those seven men chosen to serve the poor, freeing the apostles to preach the word. Stephen also serves the poor by preaching to the rich, whom he upsets by reminding them of their past and their failure to recognize God's work among them. He so infuriates some of his hearers that they stone him to death. In the Acts of the Apostles, he is described in the same way as the One whom he follows, Jesus Christ. Like his Master, he entrusts his spirit to God.

Stephen's death fulfills the Matthean Jesus' words to his disciples about being persecuted, but being filled with the Spirit of the Father as they bear witness to him. Stephen is filled with wisdom and spirit when he speaks. Both his deed (serving the poor) and his words (preaching) lead to his death. ✠

Meditation

In what ways do you serve the poor? What have been the consequences of that service?

Prayer

Lord God, you are our rock of refuge, our stronghold who gives us safety. Open our eyes to see the poor that we may serve them. Open our lips to proclaim your Word, Jesus Christ, for whom Stephen gave his life. We ask this through the same Christ, our Lord. Amen.

December 27: St. John

Hymn

O holy Child of Bethlehem!
Descend to us, we pray;
Cast out our sin and enter in;
Be born in us today.
We hear the Christmas angels
The great glad tiding tell;
O come to us, abide with us,
Our Lord Emmanuel!

"O Little Town of Bethlehem," verse 4

Reflection

The feast of St. John, apostle and evangelist, features Scripture texts attributable to St. John, namely, the First Letter of John and the Gospel of John. Both the First Letter of John and the Gospel of John begin with poetic prose that explains that Jesus Christ, the Word of life, the eternal life that always existed with the Father, was made visible as his only begotten Son, the holy Child of Bethlehem.

It is the only begotten Son who is crucified and buried in a tomb in a garden, according to John's Gospel. The tomb is found empty on the first day of the week as Simon Peter and the disciple whom Jesus loved—named by tradition as John—run to see the emptiness at Mary Magdalene's word. The beloved disciple sees the emptiness and believes in the fullness that God has raised Christ from the dead.

The One who cast out sin and descended into our world, Emmanuel—God with us—is the source of all things past, present, and future. Jesus Christ, begotten of the Father's love, created an egalitarian community, a fellowship that is shared with the Father, the Son, and the Holy Spirit by all believers forevermore. It is this unity about which St. John writes, so that all believers' joy may be complete on hearing the words of the Christmas angels and the glad tidings of the Easter angels. ✠

Meditation

How do you experience the fellowship of the Blessed Trinity?

Prayer

Father, before the beginning of time, you begot your only Son in love. As the Alpha and Omega, the source and the ending, the past, present, and future, he calls us to fellowship with you and each other. Through Jesus Christ and the Holy Spirit, with the intercession of St. John, make our unity complete forevermore. Amen.

December 28: Holy Innocents

Scriptures: 1 John 1:5–2:2; Matthew 2:13–18

Hymn

O little town of Bethlehem,
How still we see thee lie!
Above thy deep and dreamless sleep
The silent stars go by;
Yet in thy dark streets shineth
The everlasting Light;
The hopes and fears of all the years
Are met in thee tonight.

"O Little Town of Bethlehem," verse 1

Reflection

The feast of the Holy Innocents comes from the unique account in Matthew's Gospel of Herod ordering the killing of all the boys in Bethlehem and its vicinity age two years and younger after being deceived by the Magi. These Magi sought the newborn king of the Jews and were later instructed in a dream to avoid Herod, the current king who was threatened by news of the newborn babe.

While the innocent boys are being slain—much like Pharaoh once slew the baby Hebrew boys in Egypt—Joseph and Mary take Jesus to Egypt to escape Herod's command. Like Moses—who was saved from death—before Jesus, God will call his Son out of Egypt to free his people from sin.

The darkness of Herod is shattered by the light of the Child born in Bethlehem who has come to ransom the whole world, even those infants who die protecting his flight. As John writes in his first letter, "God is light, and in him there is no darkness at all" (1 John 1:5). The first verse of "O Little Town of Bethlehem" states it this way: "... [I]n thy dark streets shineth the everlasting Light." Even those who have had their light extinguished by the darkness of Herod have become light through Jesus Christ. ✠

Meditation

What darkness of yours has God scattered through Jesus Christ?

Prayer

Father, eternal light, we praise you for having ransomed us from darkness through your Son, Jesus Christ, our Advocate. Make us strong in faith, like the children martyred in Bethlehem, that we may give you glory on high through the same Jesus Christ in union with the Holy Spirit, forever and ever. Amen.

December 29:
Fifth Day in the Octave of Christmas

Scriptures: 1 John 2:3–11; Luke 2:22–35

Hymn

Silent night, holy night!
Son of God, love's pure light
Radiant beams from thy holy face
With the dawn of redeeming grace,
Jesus, Lord, at thy birth,
Jesus, Lord, at thy birth.

"Silent Night," verse 3

Reflection

Today's passage from Luke's Gospel is also read on the feast of the Presentation of the Lord (February 2), forty days after Christmas. As one of two of Jesus' childhood stories unique to Luke—the other is the story of the boy Jesus with the teachers in the Temple—two themes are present.

The first theme is that of Jesus, the Son of God, being brought to the Temple in Jerusalem to be redeemed according to the Law. Every firstborn son belongs to God; notice the wonderful Lukan irony here. Not only does Jesus belong to God as his firstborn Son but also Jesus is God incarnate. Not only do Mary and Joseph redeem Jesus with the sacrifice of two birds but also the one they redeem is the Redeemer of the world with the dawn of redeeming grace.

The second theme is light. The old man Simeon declares that he has seen love's pure light. Jesus is the light revealing the light of God to all peoples. The author of the First Letter of John also emphasizes this theme, declaring that Christians cannot hate each other and be in the light. Only authentic Christian love enables the radiant beams from Christ's holy face to shine through the lives of those who walk in the path of Jesus. ✠

Meditation

What truth do you think Luke reveals about Jesus through his presentation in the Temple? What truth do you think John reveals about Jesus in writing about him as light?

Prayer

Eternal God, your Son revealed your light to the nations and filled all people with your grace. Make us temples of your Holy Spirit, dwelling places of light, that we might not only recognize your light in others but also shine with the brilliance of Christ, who is Lord forever and ever. Amen.

December 30:
Sixth Day in the Octave of Christmas

Scriptures: 1 John 2:12–17; Luke 2:36–40

Hymn

Now to the Lord sing praises,
All you within this place,
And with true love and charity
Each other now embrace:
The merry time of Christmas
*   (alternate: This holy tide of Christmas)*
Is drawing on apace:
*   (alternate: Is filled with heavenly grace.)*
O tidings of comfort and joy, comfort and joy,
O tidings of comfort and joy!
                "God Rest You Merry, Gentlemen," verse 6

Reflection

On this sixth day in the octave of Christmas, the second half of a unique Lukan story is presented. The first half, presented on the fifth day in the octave of Christmas, provides the setting of the Temple in Jerusalem. Mary and Joseph have brought Jesus to God's house to offer two turtledoves or pigeons to fulfill the Law and ransom their firstborn son from death. First, Simeon recognizes the child as a light to all nations. Then, Anna, a prophetess, speaks about the child to whomever would listen. It is the Anna half of the story that is presented as today's Gospel passage.

Luke loves to balance a story about a man with a story about a woman. Simeon is the old man, and Anna is the old woman. Both of them recognize what others cannot see, the true love and charity of the Child Jesus. The redeemer of Israel is in their midst. His parents have presented him to his Father. The One who will ransom the world with his heavenly grace is ransomed by his parents! These are tidings of comfort and joy.

He is an ideal child, according to Luke, returning to Nazareth with his parents, growing up, becoming strong, filled with wisdom, and favored by God. In other words, as the First Letter of John states, he does not love the world or the things of the world. And as such, he is a model not only for the addressees—parents and children—of the First Letter of John but also for all who follow him. The response of his followers is to sing his praises like Simeon and Anna of old. ✣

Meditation

From what has Christ ransomed you?

Prayer

Heaven and earth rejoice in the birth of your Son, O Lord. Through his death and resurrection, you have ransomed us from sin and brought us tidings of comfort and joy. Accept our glory and praise through Lord Jesus Christ, who lives and reigns with you and the Holy Spirit, one God, forever and ever. Amen.

December 31:
Seventh Day in the Octave of Christmas

Scriptures: 1 John 2:18–21; John 1:1–18

Hymn

Joy to the world! The Lord is come;
Let earth receive her King;
Let ev'ry heart prepare Him room,
And heav'n and nature sing,
And heav'n and nature sing,
And heav'n and heav'n and nature sing.

"*Joy to the World,*" *verse 1*

Reflection

The author of the First Letter of John reminds his readers that, in this last hour, they know the truth. The prologue of John's Gospel presents in detail the truth concerning the word of God from the beginning. The spoken Word of God became incarnate of the Virgin Mary, and this continues to be celebrated from Christmas Day— with angels announcing the good news to shepherds— throughout the Christmas season, especially the eight days forming an octave.

Furthermore, the truth of John's Gospel presents the Word of God as the agent of creation, as the light that shines through all things made and overcomes darkness. At the coming of the King into the world heaven and nature sing.

John the Baptist testified to the fact that the Word incarnate was light. The Word of God came into the world as flesh and lived and walked and experienced what it was like to be a creature. In other words, the Father's only begotten Son revealed the fullness of grace and truth. He enabled those who saw him as God's light to become children of God. And he did all this even while remaining on high, that is, remaining at his Father's side. As we understand these great truths of our faith, we proclaim them joyfully to the world. ✠

Meditation

What is the greatest truth that God has revealed to you?

Prayer

Glory to you, O God, on high for revealing the truth of your word to your people. Help us to recognize your light and follow in the footsteps of your Son, Jesus Christ, whose Incarnation we celebrate. Grant us peace through him, who is at your side forever and ever. Amen.

Section VI:

Christmas Season

The feast of the Holy Family of Jesus, Mary, and Joseph
is generally celebrated on the Sunday within the octave
of Christmas—the first Sunday after Christmas—
or December 30 when there isn't a Sunday.

Holy Family, *Cycle A*

Scriptures: Sirach 3:2–7, 12–14; Colossians 3:12–21; Matthew 2:13–15, 19–23

Hymn

Holy Jesus, ev'ry day
Keep us in the narrow way;
And, when earthly things are past,
Bring our ransomed souls at last
Where they need no star to guide,
Where no clouds thy glory hide.

"As With Gladness Men of Old," verse 4

Reflection

Ancient household codes of conduct are found in the Book of Sirach and the Letter to the Colossians. A biblical household code of conduct stipulates the appropriate behavior of family members. Sirach states that children are to honor their parents, especially their father in a patriarchal culture. Colossians presents the virtues—compassion, kindness, humility, gentleness, patience, love—that are required for community family life. In either case, the codes are meant to keep people on the narrow way to eternal life.

Unique to Matthew's Gospel is the account of the trip of Jesus, Mary, and Joseph to Egypt to escape King Herod's wrath. Just as his Old Testament namesake, Joseph receives directions from God through dreams. After the Magi, who have been guided by a star, depart Bethlehem, the Holy Family moves to Egypt. Because Matthew understands

Jesus as a new Moses, Jesus' parents must take him to Egypt from which he returns, as his name suggests, to save his people from their sins, like Moses saved his people from slavery. Because Matthew had set the couple's hometown as Bethlehem, after their sojourn in Egypt he settles them in Nazareth.

Both household codes of conduct and dream revelations are biblical framers of family life. While household codes have changed, family members still need guidelines for living together in peace. These may be detailed as curfews for teenagers and bedtimes for children. Likewise, family members still need to practice the virtues of compassion, kindness, humility, gentleness, patience, and love to ensure peace in the household. All this can be held together by a vision, a dream, of what the family can be; this vision guides decisions concerning household codes and the practice of virtues. ✠

Meditation

What is your family vision? How do your household codes facilitate the vision? What virtues support the vision?

Prayer

Almighty God, through your word you teach us the importance of family life and provide us with the virtues to live in love and peace. May our vision be informed by the Holy Spirit, who lives and reigns with you and your Son, our Lord Jesus Christ, forever and ever. Amen.

Holy Family, *Cycle B*

Scriptures: Genesis 15:1–6; 21:1–3;
Hebrews 11:8, 11–12, 17–19; Luke 2:22–40

Hymn

Though an infant now we view Him,
He shall fill his Father's throne,
Gather all the nations to Him;
Ev'ry knee shall then bow down:
Come and worship, come and worship,
Worship Christ, the newborn King.

"Angels, from the Realms of Glory," verse 4

Reflection

Simeon makes a unique cameo appearance in today's
Gospel passage. Like others throughout Luke's first two
chapters, he is guided by the Holy Spirit to the Temple
when Mary and Joseph bring Jesus there to present him to
the Lord. The Holy Spirit inspires old Simeon to take the
infant in his hands and declare that salvation has come to
all lands, both for Gentiles and Jews.

Once upon a time in human history, God had chosen
Abraham and Sarah and promised them descendants
as numerous as the stars in the sky. Trusting the Lord,
Abraham left his country, not knowing where he was going,
to a land God promised him. When Abraham and Sarah
had no heir, the Lord gave them Isaac. When Abraham was
put to the test, he was ready to offer Isaac in sacrifice to
God, whom he trusted could raise the dead to new life.

The countless descendants of Abraham and Sarah—known successively as Hebrews, Israelites, and Jews—are the recipients of God's glory, according to joy-filled Simeon. All other people, known as Gentiles, are recipients of revelation, according to old Simeon. All lands, all peoples, all nations have been chosen by the Lord to form one holy family of God's people. What Simeon declares to be a reality remains a goal to be achieved. ✠

Meditation

What can you do to realize the goal of one holy family of God's people?

Prayer

God of Abraham and Sarah, of Joseph and Mary, of Simeon and Anna, through your Holy Spirit and the birth of your Son, you reveal your salvation goal of the unity of all people in one holy family. Remove the darkness that blinds us from achieving your goal. You are one God—Father, Son, and Holy Spirit—forever and ever. Amen.

Holy Family, *Cycle C*

Scriptures: 1 Samuel 1:20–22, 24–28;
1 John 3:1–2, 21–24; Luke 2:41–52

Hymn

He rules the world with truth and grace,
And makes the nations prove
The glories of His righteousness,
And wonders of His love,
And wonders of His love,
And wonders, wonders of His love.

"Joy to the World," verse 4

Reflection

The Sunday between Christmas and January 1 is the feast of the Holy Family of Jesus, Mary, and Joseph. The passage from Luke's Gospel is the second of two of Jesus' childhood stories—the other is the Presentation in the Temple—that are unique to Luke.

As a twelve-year-old boy, Jesus journeys with his parents to Jerusalem for the annual spring festival of Passover, the feast that recalls God's liberation of his people from Egyptian slavery. When his parents head home after the feast, the boy hangs back and remains for three days in Jerusalem, while his parents notice that he is missing from the caravan heading home and search for him. When they find him, he is conversing with the teachers in the Temple.

This scene, of course, prefigures the future dialogues he will have with the teachers in the Temple during his year of ministry. It displays his righteousness, his healthy relationship with God.

The passage from the First Book of Samuel portrays Elkanah and Hannah fulfilling their promise to bring their miracle child Samuel to the shrine at Shiloh and present him to the priest Eli. The covenant made between the post-child-bearing-years couple and God was that Samuel would be dedicated to the Lord if they conceived a son. Second only to Moses in the Hebrew Bible (Old Testament), Samuel becomes a judge, a priest, a prophet, and an anointer of kings.

As God's children, all now behold him ruling the world with truth and grace. The long-expected Lord, prefigured by prophets like Samuel, fulfills God's word. All that people, his redeemed family, can do is praise him together as one for the wonders of his love. ✠

Meditation

What does it mean for you to be a member of God's holy family?

Prayer

God of all, you created the family of Jesus, Mary, and Joseph to reveal holiness in the world. Grant that we, your redeemed people, may overflow with your grace and praise you as Father, Son, and Holy Spirit, forever and ever. Amen.

January 1: Mary, the Holy Mother of God

This Holy Day of Obligation and solemnity is celebrated every year on January 1, the octave (eighth) day of Christmas. The obligation is removed when January 1 falls on a Saturday or a Monday.

Scriptures: Numbers 6:22–27; Galatians 4:4–7; Luke 2:16–21

Hymn

What child is this, who laid to rest,
On Mary's lap is sleeping?
Whom angels greet with anthems sweet,
While shepherds watch are keeping?
This, this is Christ the King,
Whom shepherds guard and angels sing;
Haste, haste to bring him laud,
The Babe, the son of Mary.

"What Child Is This," verse 1

Reflection

The eighth day of Christmas, the Solemnity of Mary, the Holy Mother of God, presents multiple themes for consideration. The first is found in the title for the celebration. God's Son was born of a woman; the Babe, the son of Mary, is God. Therefore, she is the Mother of God.

The Gospel passage that was begun at Christmas Mass during the night is finished eight days later. Luke uniquely narrates the story about shepherds keeping the night watch over their sheep, receiving the revelation that God's Son has been born in Bethlehem, and the shepherds hasten to go there and recognize the truth of the good news that had been delivered to them by an angel chorus. Their response to finding the child at rest on Mary's lap is to amaze others with their message.

For the Infant Christ the King to ransom those born under the Law, he must submit himself to the Law. And so on the eighth day he is incorporated into God's chosen people through circumcision and given his name, Jesus, which Gabriel had announced to the Virgin of Nazareth before he was conceived in her womb.

The blessings promised by the Lord to Moses and spoken of by Aaron the priest are fulfilled in the Nativity of the Lord. God's face now shines on all, who hasten to praise him, like the shepherds and the angels. ✠

Meditation

What theme on this eighth day of Christmas speaks most eloquently to you? Why?

Prayer

Abba, Father, through the gift of your Holy Spirit you enable us to laud your name. Grant us your blessing, let your face shine on us, be gracious to us, and give us peace through your Son, Jesus Christ, who lives and reigns with you and the Holy Spirit, one God, forever and ever. Amen.

January 2

Scriptures: 1 John 2:22–28; John 1:19–28

Hymn

Christ by highest heav'n adored;
Christ the everlasting Lord!
Late in time behold Him come,
Offspring of the Virgin's womb:
Veiled in flesh the Godhead see;
Hail th' incarnate Deity,
Pleased as man with us to dwell,
Jesus, our Emmanuel.
Hark! the herald angels sing,
"Glory to the newborn King!"

"Hark! The Herald Angels Sing," verse 2

Reflection

The First Letter of John names as a liar anyone who denies that Jesus is the Christ, that is, the anointed of God, the everlasting Lord. Jesus, offspring of the Virgin's womb, is the incarnate Deity, the Godhead, veiled in human flesh. The author of the First Letter of John urges his readers to remain in this truth.

According to John's Gospel, John the Baptist had testified to this long before. The Baptizer made it clear that he was not the Christ, nor Elijah returned, nor Isaiah the prophet returned. John was the herald of the One adored in heaven, Christ the everlasting Lord, who was coming into the world. The Word of God became flesh and was pleased to dwell on earth with all of creation. In his person, Jesus was Emmanuel, God-with-people.

Jesus Christ, who invites all to remain in him, promises eternal life. The second person of the Holy Trinity unites all those he has anointed in himself through the Spirit and presents them to the Father, who is eternal life. Thus, all remain in all; all dwell in life eternally. ✤

Meditation

What saving deed does God accomplish through you because you remain in Jesus Christ?

Prayer

Father of our Lord Jesus Christ, through the Incarnation you made your Son human and offered all people the gift of eternal life. Grant us the grace to recognize Emmanuel in all we meet and share in the same eternal life. All glory be yours, Father, Son, and Holy Spirit, forever and ever. Amen.

January 3

Scriptures: 1 John 2:29–3:6; John 1:29–34

Hymn

Hail, the heav'n born Prince of Peace!
Hail the Sun of Righteousness!
Light and life to all He brings,
Ris'n with healing in His wings.
Mild He lays his glory by,
Born that we may no more may die,
Born to raise us from the earth,
Born to give us second birth.
Hark! the herald angels sing,
"Glory to the newborn King!"

"Hark! The Herald Angels Sing," verse 3

Reflection

Not only does every person have a name—or two or three—but people also give names to everything, such as dogs, cats, homes, and cars. Knowing the name of a person gives one the power to call him or her. The name Jesus—meaning "God saves"—not only honors the man who bore it but it also illustrates the many other names by which people call on the Son of God.

The third verse of "Hark! The Herald Angels Sing" names Jesus as the heaven-born Prince of Peace, the Sun of Righteousness, and the newborn King. The name, Sun of Righteousness, echoes the passage from the First Letter of John, which refers to God as righteous, meaning that all is right with God. Those who act out of a right relationship with God are declared to be righteous by John. That makes them children of God.

In the selection from John's Gospel, John the Baptist names Jesus as the Lamb of God, who takes away the sin of the world. He is the sacrifice that restores people's relationship with God. At every Mass, while the eucharistic bread is broken, the people sing: "Lamb of God, you take away the sins of the world, have mercy on us." The bread, the Body of Christ, has been sacrificed in an unbloody manner. By receiving it, people's relationship with God is restored, that is, the risen Christ brings light and life to all who receive him.

In his Incarnation, he set aside his glory and became flesh, born that people may no longer die. Through his death, he destroyed death. Though his resurrection, he has raised all from the earth and given all a second birth. We now join the heavenly heralds during this Christmas season, singing praise of his name: "Glory to the newborn King!" ✠

Meditation

What is the meaning of your name(s)?

Prayer

Almighty Father, you bestowed your saving name upon your only begotten Son, Jesus. As we honor his name, at whom all in heaven, on earth, and under the earth bow, grant us a share in the eternal feast of heaven. We ask this through the Lamb of God, who lives and reigns with you and the Holy Spirit, forever and ever Amen.

January 4

Scriptures: 1 John 3:7–10; John 1:35–42

Hymn

God rest you merry, gentlemen,
Let nothing you dismay,
Remember Christ our Savior
Was born on Christmas Day
To save us all from Satan's pow'r
When we were gone astray:
O tidings of comfort and joy, comfort and joy,
O tidings of comfort and joy!
"God Rest You Merry, Gentlemen," verse 1

Reflection

In the passage from John's Gospel, Jesus invites two of John the Baptist's disciples to follow him and see where he is staying. One of those two disciples is Andrew, who, imitating Jesus, finds his brother Simon and tells him that they have found the Messiah, which means Christ, Anointed. The selection from the First Letter of John indicates that this is an act of righteousness, that is, it is done out of a healthy relationship with God. The person who acts in righteousness is righteous, just as Jesus Christ is righteous, just as those who answer his call are righteous.

We have heard the call to enter into a relationship with God. Any relationship involves cooperation between those involved in it. God makes the first move and offers friendship through Christ, born on Christmas Day because we had gone astray. We respond to God's offer and experience comfort and joy. Our response means that we are willing to cooperate with God; in the words of the First Letter of John, we act in righteousness, that is, our deeds flow out of our right relationship with God. A healthy relationship with God provides the means for us to hear the call and permit God to accomplish his work through us. ✠

Meditation

In righteousness, what do you think God is accomplishing in your life?

Prayer

As we continue to celebrate this Christmas season, O God, remembering the birth of your Son that saved us from Satan's power when we had strayed, we ask that you give us rest, comfort, and joy. Through our Lord Jesus Christ, your Son, who lives and reigns with you and the Holy Spirit, one God, forever and ever. Amen.

January 5

Scriptures: 1 John 3:11–21; John 1:43–51

Hymn

No more let sins and sorrows grow,
Nor thorns infest the ground;
He comes to make His blessings flow
Far as the curse is found,
Far as the curse is found,
Far as, far as the curse is found.

"Joy to the World," verse 3

Reflection

The third verse of "Joy to the World" understands Christmas to be a reversal of God's curse on the earth after the first man and woman disobeyed God. Instead of the earth yielding thorns, now it brings forth blessings through the birth of Jesus Christ.

The passage from the First Letter of John illustrates one of the results of the curse: Cain killing his brother, Abel. Those who follow Christ reverse this deed by loving one another, even if the world hates them for it. Authentic love brings about the death of the ego so that the other person is placed ahead of the beloved.

The passage from John's Gospel demonstrates this in action. Jesus invited Philip to follow him; Philip, setting aside his own interests in love, seeks Nathaniel and invites him to follow Jesus. One disciple's response in love to Jesus propels him to invite another. Likewise, wherever we go, we invite others to follow Christ in love. ✠

Meditation

In what ways do you invite others to follow Christ in love?

Prayer

Through the birth of your Son, Almighty Father, you have removed the ancient curse and opened the floodgates of your grace. As we keep this Christmas festival, strengthen your blessing of love in us, that we may invite others to follow Jesus Christ, who lives and reigns with you and the Holy Spirit, one God, forever and ever. Amen.

January 6

Scriptures: 1 John 5:5–13; Mark 1:7–11 or Luke 3:23–38

Hymn

Sing, choirs of angels, sing in exultation,
Sing all ye citizens of heav'n above:
"Glory to God, glory in the highest:"
O come, let us adore Him,
O come, let us adore Him,
O come, let us adore Him, Christ the Lord!

"O Come, All Ye Faithful," verse 6

Reflection

The great and mighty wonder of Christmas continues with Luke's unique genealogy of Jesus. More familiar is Matthew's genealogy, found at the beginning of his Gospel, that traces Jesus' human line from Abraham to David to the Babylonian exile to Christ, conveniently divided into three sets of fourteen generations. Luke presents a different genealogy, beginning with Jesus, who was thought to be the son of Joseph, and tracing his human line back through twenty-five generations to Adam, the first son of God. Luke has already narrated how the Virgin of Nazareth, Mary, conceived in her womb God's Word by the power of the Holy Spirit and gave birth to him in Bethlehem. For Luke, Jesus is doubly the Son of God, by Spirit and by lineage.

The First Letter of John also bears testimony to Jesus' human manifestation. Using key Johannine words, the letter declares that Jesus Christ came into the world through Spirit, water, and blood. The Spirit is God's truth, God's testimony that Jesus Christ is his Son. The water is life, eternal life begun with baptism. And the blood is the sacrificial death of God's own Son on the cross in which people share through the Eucharist.

According to the First Letter of John, whoever believes the testimony of Spirit, water, and blood possesses eternal life. According to Luke, whoever believes that Jesus is the Son of God is offered the kingdom of God. These truths should be enough to prompt all citizens of heaven to sing, "Glory to God, glory in the highest," and adore Christ the Lord. ✠

Meditation

Which image from today's Scripture texts gets your attention? Why?

Prayer

Ever-living God, during this Christmas season we rejoice with heart and soul and voice that you have saved us through the birth of your Son, Jesus Christ. Hear our prayer and give us ever greater confidence in him who calls us to everlasting life. He lives and reigns with you and the Holy Spirit, one God, forever and ever. Amen.

January 7

Scriptures: 1 John 5:14–21; John 2:1–11

Hymn

Good Christians all, rejoice
With heart and soul and voice!
Now ye need not fear the grave;
Jesus Christ was born to save!
Calls you one and calls you all
To gain his everlasting hall.
Christ was born to save!
Christ was born to save!

"Good Christians All, Rejoice," verse 3

Reflection

The word "confidence" comes from the union of two Latin words: con, meaning "with," and fide, meaning "faith." Thus, confidence means "with faith" or "with trust." The First Letter of John urges confidence in God, that if we ask anything according to his will, he hears us. Confidence is also demonstrated in the passage from John's Gospel. Jesus, attending a wedding reception, finds out from his mother that the guests have consumed all the wine. He tells the servers to fill six stone jars with water and dip some out and take it to the headwaiter. The servers confidently do what he tells them, and discover that the water has become wine.

Confidence is hard to possess, because many people disappoint us. A friend says that she will pick up our mail while we are out of town for a few days. When we return, we discover the mailbox overflowing with magazines, bills, and junk. Another friend promises to return a book after borrowing and reading it. A few years later, while hunting for it, we discover that it has never been returned. A bank employee or business associate or another person assures us that a mistake has been corrected. But the next bank statement or bill or whatever has the same error as before. This confidence we lose in others is transferred to God.

The First Letter of John tells us to seek God's will for us and to have confidence that God hears us in regard to whatever we ask. John presents a very important caveat, however. Our confidence does not rest in our own determination as to what we need, such as in telling God what he needs to do. Our confidence rests in God giving us what we need to do his will. Our trust is that through our prayer God will direct our wills to doing his. As we develop this confidence, we also come to understand that we do not fear the grave, because Jesus Christ was born to save us. ✚

~~~~~~

Meditation

What recent event in your life called forth great confidence in God from you?

~~~~~~

Prayer

Ever-living God, during this Christmas season we rejoice with heart and soul and voice that you have saved us through the birth of your Son, Jesus Christ. Hear our prayer and give us ever greater confidence in him who calls us to everlasting life. He lives and reigns with you and the Holy Spirit, one God, forever and ever. Amen.

Section VII:
Epiphany

✠

This solemnity is celebrated on the Sunday between January 2 and January 8.

Solemnity: The Epiphany of the Lord

Scriptures: Isaiah 60:1–6; Ephesians 3:2–3a, 5–6; Matthew 2:1–2

Hymn

We three kings of Orient are,
Bearing gifts we traverse afar,
Field and fountain,
Moor and mountain,
Following yonder star.
O star of wonder, star of night,
Star with royal beauty bright
Westward leading,
Still proceeding,
Guide us to thy perfect light!

"We Three Kings of Orient Are," verse 1

Reflection

Today's Gospel does not mention the "three kings of Orient," as does the first verse of "We Three Kings of Orient Are." The passage from Matthew's Gospel merely states that Magi from the east sought the newborn king of the Jews to offer him the three gifts of gold, frankincense, and myrrh. Both the carol and the Gospel focus on the light that the Magi follow to the "perfect light," Jesus Christ.

Light is also the topic of the prophet Isaiah. Exhorting the returning Jewish exiles from Babylon not to be depressed by the ruins that had once been Jerusalem and the Temple, Isaiah invites the city to rise up in splendor because light has come; the Lord shines on his people again. While other peoples (Gentiles) are in darkness, the Jews are bathed in light.

The Letter to the Ephesians explains that the Light, Jesus Christ, now shines on all peoples. Echoing Matthew's Magi, Paul declares that Gentiles are now coheirs, members of the same body through faith in God's only begotten Son. While Paul's new understanding does not upset modern people like it would ancient Jews, some people remain in darkness. They need modern Magi bearing the gift of the good news that God has chosen all people to be his people. ✠

Meditation

In what ways are you a gift-bearer of God's good news to others?

Prayer

Lord Jesus, you are the perfect light that all people seek. As we journey through this life, make us faithful followers and proclaimers of the good news of what your Father has done. At the end of our pilgrimage, guide us to the eternal light of heaven, where you live and reign with the Father and the Holy Spirit, one God, forever and ever. Amen.

Monday After Epiphany *or* January 7

Scriptures: 1 John 3:22 – 4:6;
Matthew 4:12–17, 23–25

Hymn

*As with gladness men of old
Did the guiding star behold,
As with joy they hailed its light,
Leading onward, beaming bright,
So, most gracious God, may we
Evermore be led to thee.*

"As With Gladness Men of Old," verse 1

Reflection

The journey through Christmas continues for one more week. The First Letter of John explains the difference between the spirit of truth and the spirit of deceit. The spirit of truth prompts hearers to believe in the name of Jesus Christ and to remain in him. The spirit of truth tells people that Jesus Christ belongs to God. It also sparks love among the members of the community.

The spirit of deceit leads hearers away from Jesus Christ and to the things of the world. Those who follow the spirit of deceit do not believe in Jesus Christ. They do not think that he came in the flesh. And they do not love one another. Because both spirits exist, it is of the utmost importance that every spirit be tested so that one can be sure that he or she is listening to God and being led to him.

In the midst of darkness, Jesus emerges in Matthew's Gospel proclaiming the light of the kingdom of heaven. The response of those who heard his words and witnessed his enacting of the kingdom through curing every disease and illness among the people is repentance—or in the words of the First Letter of John, the testing of spirits. Repentance means to turn 180 degrees in one's journey. Like the Magi of old, those who repent follow the light of a star that is not of this world. It leads them onward throughout their lives in the kingdom of heaven here and into the fullness of that kingdom on the other side of death. ✠

Meditation

What process do you use to determine the difference between the spirit of truth and the spirit of deceit?

Prayer

O God who guided the Magi by the light of a star to your Son, Jesus Christ, and hailing its light, they journeyed onward to find the newborn king of the Jews: Fill us with your Holy Spirit that we may separate the spirit of truth from the spirit of deceit and be led to the fullness of the kingdom of heaven, where you live as one God, forever and ever. Amen.

Tuesday After Epiphany *or* January 8

Scriptures: 1 John 4:7–10; Mark 6:34–44

Hymn

Yea, Lord, we greet thee, born this happy morning,
Jesus, to thee be all glory giv'n;
Word of the Father now in flesh appearing:
O come, let us adore Him,
O come, let us adore Him,
O come, let us adore Him, Christ the Lord!

"O Come, All Ye Faithful," verse 7

Reflection

The theme of epiphany, or the manifestation of God or God's enfleshment, continues to be illustrated in the Scripture texts assigned for today. Jesus is love incarnate, love divine. He is the manifestation or enfleshment of God, who was born on Christmas morning. As the First Letter of John makes so clear, it is not that people loved God, but that God loved people and sent his love into the world in the person of Jesus Christ.

Not only was Jesus Christ the sign of God's love but also his signs manifested God's love, otherwise called the kingdom of heaven. Today's passage from Mark's Gospel presents the epiphany of twelve wicker baskets of leftover bread and fish. Five loaves and two fish feed 5,000 men after Jesus takes, blesses, breaks, and gives them to his disciples to set before the people. God had once fed his Chosen People in the desert with manna; Jesus manifests God's kingdom by feeding his disciples in a deserted place.

This epiphanic sign is witnessed by many every day when they celebrate the Eucharist or participate in Mass. In other words, the response to the epiphany is worship, the adoration of the God who incarnated himself, the adoration of the God who entered the world in the person of his only begotten Son, the adoration of the God who feeds his people with heavenly bread. O come, let us adore him. ✠

Meditation

What is your response to God's epiphanies?

Prayer

We worship you, O Lord, one God of three persons. We praise you, Father, for your wisdom in sending your divine love, Jesus Christ, into the world. We ask for your Holy Spirit to help us recognize your epiphanies or manifestations this day. You live and reign as one God—Father, Son, and Holy Spirit—forever and ever. Amen.

Wednesday After Epiphany *or* January 9

Scriptures: 1 John 4:11–18; Mark 6:45–52

Hymn

For Christ is born of Mary;
And gathered all above,
While mortal sleep, the angels keep
Their watch of wond'ring love.
O morning stars, together
Proclaim the holy birth;
And praises sing to God the King,
And peace to all on earth.

"O Little Town of Bethlehem," verse 2

Reflection

Love is an overused word; it can mean anything and everything. The love written about by John in his first letter, however, is sacrificial love. This wondering love puts another ahead of oneself; this type of love gets one's ego out of the way so that one's self is put at the disposal of the beloved, like the angels keeping watch over the holy birth of Jesus. The First Letter of John identifies God as being sacrificial love, because God loved people first, and for no reason except that the Creator wanted to experience what it was like to be a creature. Thus, love became flesh in the person of Jesus Christ, God's only begotten Son, born of Mary.

When people love one another sacrificially, they are epiphanies, manifestations, of God's love. Those who love sacrificially remain in God and God in them, and love brings them to perfection. Sacrificial love contains no fear, because perfect sacrificial love drives out fear just like Jesus drove out fear in his disciples, when they were in the boat tossed about by the wind and the sea.

In the midst of a crisis or chaos or accident, or anything else that causes people to doubt, Jesus comes walking on the disturbance and calms it and brings peace to those experiencing a lack of trust. Epiphanies occur everywhere for those who remain in love. If one's heart is hardened, however, and one thinks that he or she must save himself or herself, fear sets in. Such a person is not yet perfect in love. Sacrificial love elicits an absolute trust in God, which results in praises for the heavenly King. ✛

Meditation

In what ways is sacrificial love your plea, your gift, and your sign?

Prayer

God of love, you manifested sacrificial love in the person of your Son, Jesus Christ, the Savior of the world, the One who has given us your Spirit of love. Draw us deeper and deeper in your divine love, that it may come to perfection in us and we may share in it completely in the kingdom, where you live and reign, forever and ever. Amen.

Thursday After Epiphany *or* January 10

Scriptures: 1 John 4:19—5:4; Luke 4:14–22

Hymn

So bring Him incense, gold and myrrh,
Come, peasant, king to own Him;
The King of kings salvation brings,
Let loving hearts enthrone Him.
This, this is Christ the King,
Whom shepherds guard and angels sing;
Haste, haste to bring Him laud,
The Babe, the son of Mary.

"What Child Is This," verse 3

Reflection

A ransom is a price paid for the redemption of a captured person. According to John's first letter, God loved people and decided to ransom them from sin and death. The price paid was the Incarnation of God's only begotten Son, the infant born in Bethlehem, the King of kings who received incense, gold, and myrrh. Jesus taught people to love one another in the same way that God manifests his love, namely, sacrificially. A person cannot say that he or she loves God unless he or she also loves others.

Sacrificial love does not own or possess another. Sacrificial love frees the other person to be who he or she is, a unique child of God. Not only did God not own Jesus but he also set him free in a body—Incarnation—so that he could love others and demonstrate the depth of his love by dying on a cross.

This freeing love is proclaimed by Jesus in Luke's Gospel. Isaiah's passage about good news and liberty to captives, recovery of sight for the blind, and freedom for the oppressed is fulfilled in the preaching and ministry of Jesus of Nazareth. He is the enfleshment of love that sets others free. He is the epiphany or manifestation of freeing love. Those who believe that Jesus is the Christ are begotten by God in love and freed to love as God loves. ✠

Meditation

In what specific ways do you love others as God loves you? In what specific ways is this a freeing love?

Prayer

All glory be to you on high, O God, who bring peace to all on earth through the Incarnation and epiphany of the infant born in Bethlehem, your Son, Jesus Christ. Through the freeing love he shares with you and the Holy Spirit, he ransomed us from sin and death and taught us to love sacrificially, just as he loved us to his death on the cross. Grant us a share in this divine love, through the same Christ, our Lord. Amen.

Friday After Epiphany *or* January 11

Hymn

Good Christians all, rejoice
With heart and soul and voice!
Now ye hear of endless bliss;
Jesus Christ was born for this!
He has opened heaven's door,
and we are blest forevermore.
Christ was born for this!
Christ was born for this!

"Good Christians All, Rejoice," verse 2

Reflection

The second verse of "Good Christians All, Rejoice" summarizes the passage from the First Letter of John. Christians rejoice with heart and soul and voice because God gave them eternal life in his Son, Jesus Christ. The hymn refers to this as endless bliss. The purpose of the Incarnation was to manifest through Spirit, water, and blood the eternal life that God desired for all people from the foundation of the world.

The passage from Luke's Gospel manifests this bliss or eternal life breaking into the world through Jesus' enactment of the kingdom of God by touching and healing a leper. The man, who was ostracized because of his leprosy, is restored to the community by Jesus' touch and healing. Jesus incurs the uncleanness of the leper by touching him; this uncleanness will later ostracize him and lead to his death on the cross.

Another metaphor in the hymn is that of opening the door. Through his death and resurrection, Jesus has opened heaven's door, and people are blessed forevermore. That was the purpose of his Incarnation. That is what was manifested in his epiphany. ✣

Meditation

What are some modern signs of eternal life or endless bliss?

Prayer

Through the birth and epiphany of your Son, O Lord, you have caused all Christians to rejoice with heart and soul and voice. Lead us through heaven's door, that we may share endless bliss with you and Jesus Christ, and the Holy Spirit, and be blessed forevermore. We ask this through the same Christ, our Lord. Amen.

Saturday After Epiphany *or* January 12

Scriptures: 1 John 5:14–21; John 3:22–30

Hymn

Manifest in making whole
Trembling limbs and fainting soul;
Manifest in valiant fight,
Quelling all the devil's might;
Manifest in gracious will,
Ever bringing good from ill;
Anthems be to thee addressed,
God in flesh made manifest.

"Songs of Thankfulness and Praise," verse 3

Reflection

On this second-to-last day of the Christmas season, the third verse of "Songs of Thankfulness and Praise" summarizes the past week of epiphanies. Jesus has been manifest in making whole the trembling limbs of the diseased and the fainting soul of a leper. He has been manifest in his gracious will to feed 5,000 men with five loaves and two fish and to save his disciples when they were tossed about by the wind and the sea. He has been manifest in bringing good from ill by announcing the time of fulfillment.

The hymn also echoes the First Letter of John's words about the evil one. Jesus has been manifest in the valiant fight against evil. He has quelled all the devil's might. He has revealed that those begotten by God through the waters of baptism are protected by God. Belonging to God, they cannot be touched by the evil one, and they know that Jesus is the Son of God. All who are baptized are in the One who is true and in his Son, Jesus Christ. John the Baptist prepared the way for his epiphany and began to decrease so that he could increase. Jesus is the true God who has come down from heaven to share with all humankind the very life—eternal—he enjoys with God. ✣

Meditation

In what ways do you experience the manifestation of eternal life now?

Prayer

Ever-living God, you manifest yourself in the flesh of your Son, Jesus Christ, and in all those whom you have begotten through water and the Holy Spirit. Protect us from the evil one and give us a share in eternal life. We ask this through our Lord Jesus Christ, who lives and reigns with you and the Holy Spirit, one God, forever and ever. Amen.

Baptism of the Lord, *Cycle A*

*This feast is celebrated on the Sunday after January 6,
or when Epiphany falls on January 7 or January 8, on
the Monday immediately following. It marks the end
of the Christmas season liturgically, and it is the first
Sunday in Ordinary Time.*

Scriptures: Isaiah 42:1–4, 6–7; Acts 10:34–38;
Matthew 3:13–17

Hymn

Joy to the world! the Lord is come;
Let earth receive her King;
Let ev'ry heart prepare Him room,
And heav'n and nature sing,
And heav'n and nature sing,
And heav'n and heav'n and nature sing.

"Joy to the World!" verse 1

Reflection

In Matthew's account of Jesus' baptism, John the
Baptist uniquely tries to prevent it, declaring that he needs
to be baptized by Jesus. Jesus, however, tells him to do it to
fulfill all righteousness, and John baptizes the Lord, who
has come into the world. The fulfillment-of-righteousness
theme in Matthew's Gospel indicates a healthy relationship
with God. To demonstrate that Jesus and God have a good
relationship, God's Spirit descends on him at his baptism,
and God declares, "This is my Son, the Beloved, with whom
I am well pleased" (Matthew 3:17).

The selection from Peter's speech to Cornelius and the members of his household in the Acts of the Apostles emphasizes the same point. Peter has just witnessed the Spirit come on the Gentiles; this leads him to conclude that God shows no partiality to the Jews. Anyone who acts uprightly, that is in righteousness, anyone who prepares room for God in his or her heart is acceptable to God. Isaiah, too, writes about this topic, presenting the servant of the Lord, the one with whom God is pleased, the one who brings the victory of justice, as the result of a healthy relationship with God.

Baptism begins a healthy relationship with God. The righteousness that baptism begins, however, like the beginning of any other relationship, must be nourished. It requires commitment. There is nothing magical about it. Just as Jesus' baptism launched his mission of proclaiming God's kingdom, so our baptism launched our mission of relating to God to fulfill all righteousness. ✠

Meditation

What steps have you taken recently to deepen your relationship with God?

Prayer

Heaven and nature sing at the wonders witnessed at the Jordan River, heavenly Father. Grant that we might hear the echo of your majestic voice over the waters of our lives as we live in righteousness. Through our Lord Jesus Christ, your Son, who lives and reigns with you and the Holy Spirit, one God, forever and ever. Amen.

Baptism of the Lord, *Cycle B*

Scriptures: Isaiah 55:1-11; 1 John 5:1-9; Mark 1:7-11

Hymn

Grant us grace to see thee, Lord,
Present in thy holy Word;
Grace to imitate thee now
And be pure, as pure art thou;
That we might become like thee
At thy great epiphany,
And may praise thee, ever blest,
God in flesh made manifest.

"Songs of Thankfulness and Praise," verse 4

Reflection

In the prophet Isaiah, God compares the word that goes forth from his mouth to rain and snow that come down from the heavens. The rain and snow water the earth, making it fertile and fruitful; God's word waters people, making them do his will, making them achieve his end. Those who are thirsty should come to this water.

In Mark's Gospel, Jesus, God in flesh made manifest, comes to the water of the Jordan to be baptized by John the Baptizer, who is proclaiming that one coming after him will baptize with the Holy Spirit. After he is plunged into the water that makes things fertile and fruitful, he has an epiphany. He sees the heavens torn open and the Spirit descending on him. Then, he hears God's word, "You are my Son, the Beloved; with you I am well pleased" (Mark 1:11).

After this he will proceed to achieve the end for which God sent him into the world, namely, the cross, referred to by the First Letter of John as blood.

For us, God's word is like rain and snow falling from the heavens. Every Sunday we hear four passages of God's word: one from a prophet, one from a psalm, one from an apostle, and one from a gospel. Daily, we have the opportunity to hear three selections from God's word at Mass or on our own as often as we want. That word waters us. That word graces us, making us fertile and fruitful, providing the opportunity for an epiphany, a manifestation of God. That word sends us on mission, just like Jesus' baptism launched his work in Galilee. ✠

Meditation

What particular Scripture passage is like rain and snow falling from the heavens on you? Explain.

Prayer

Because your ways are above our ways and your thoughts are above our thoughts, O Lord, you water us with words from your mouth. Grant us the grace to recognize your presence in those words, that we may do your will and praise you, Father, Son, and Holy Spirit, forever and ever. Amen.

Baptism of the Lord, *Cycle C*

Scriptures: Isaiah 40:1-5, 9-11; Titus 2:11-14; 3:4-7; Luke 3:15-16, 21-22

Hymn

> *Manifest in Jordan's stream*
> *Prophet, Priest, and King supreme;*
> *And at Cana wedding guest*
> *In thy Godhead manifest;*
> *Manifest in pow'r divine,*
> *Changing water into wine;*
> *Anthems be to thee addressed,*
> *God in flesh made manifest.*
>
> "Songs of Thankfulness and Praise," verse 2

Reflection

The words of the biblical texts take on new meaning in light of this feast of the Baptism of the Lord. "See, the Lord God comes with might," writes Isaiah (40:10). "The grace of God has appeared," states the Letter to Titus (2:11). And Luke's Gospel identifies the power of God and the grace of God as Jesus, manifested in the Jordan River as prophet, priest, and king. His bath of rebirth and renewal by the Holy Spirit is poured on all who believe what the voice from heaven proclaims to Jesus: "You are my Son, the Beloved; with you I am well pleased" (Luke 3:22).

There are two unique features to Luke's account of Jesus' baptism. The first is that John the Baptist is absent; he has been arrested and imprisoned. Thus, it is unknown who baptizes Jesus. Second, Jesus is praying when the heaven is opened and the Holy Spirit descends on him in bodily form like a dove. The one who was conceived by the overshadowing of the Holy Spirit is filled even more with the Spirit, who will guide his ministry throughout the rest of the Gospel.

God is manifest in the flesh. Here is God! God is manifest in the Jordan River. Here is God! The celebration of the Lord's baptism is not about an event of the past; it is about the events taking place here and now. Even as all await the blessed hope, the appearance of the glory of our great God and savior Jesus Christ, proclaimed at every Mass, God is manifest in our lives now. When an appearance of grace is realized, all people can do is praise God with an anthem of praise. ✤

Meditation

What recent appearance of God has occurred in your life? How did you praise God in response?

Prayer

All-holy God, the one mightier than John the Baptist was manifested in the Jordan River, as you declared him to be your beloved Son with whom you were well-pleased. Grant that we who have been baptized into him may live temperately, justly, and devoutly in this age, as we await the blessed hope, the appearance of the glory of our great God and Savior, Jesus Christ. He is Lord forever and ever. Amen.

Index of Hymns
Alphabetical by Title or First Line

Angels, from the Realms of Glory
As with Gladness Men of Old
Come, Holy Ghost
Come, Thou Long Expected Jesus
Creator of the Stars of Night
God Rest You Merry, Gentlemen
Good Christians, All, Rejoice
Good King Wenceslas
Go, Tell It on the Mountain
Hark! The Herald Angels Sing
It Came Upon the Midnight Clear
Joy to the World
Lo, How a Rose E'er Blooming
O Come, All Ye Faithful
O Come, O Come, Emmanuel
O Little Town of Bethlehem
On Jordan's Bank the Baptist's Cry
Silent Night
Songs of Thankfulness and Praise
The Coming of Our God
The First Nowell
Wake, Awake! For Night Is Flying
We Three Kings of Orient Are
What Child Is This

CPSIA information can be obtained
at www.ICGtesting.com
Printed in the USA
BVHW04s1310151018
530226BV00013B/170/P

9 780764 825248